# The Look of
# Old Time WASHINGTON

# The Look of Old Time WASHINGTON

Lucile McDonald &
Werner Lenggenhager

## SUPERIOR PUBLISHING COMPANY
## SEATTLE

*Printed in The United States of America*
*Graphic Arts Center, Portland, Oregon*

CASHMERE PIONEER VILLAGE.

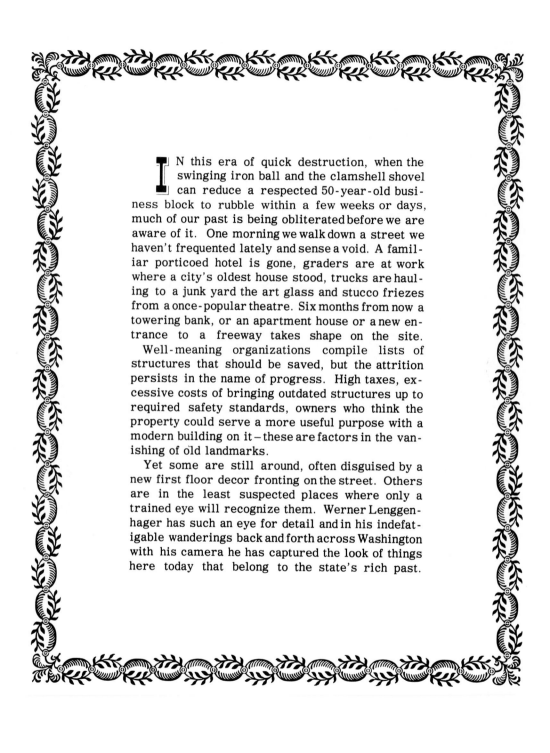

I N this era of quick destruction, when the swinging iron ball and the clamshell shovel can reduce a respected 50-year-old business block to rubble within a few weeks or days, much of our past is being obliterated before we are aware of it. One morning we walk down a street we haven't frequented lately and sense a void. A familiar porticoed hotel is gone, graders are at work where a city's oldest house stood, trucks are hauling to a junk yard the art glass and stucco friezes from a once-popular theatre. Six months from now a towering bank, or an apartment house or a new entrance to a freeway takes shape on the site.

Well-meaning organizations compile lists of structures that should be saved, but the attrition persists in the name of progress. High taxes, excessive costs of bringing outdated structures up to required safety standards, owners who think the property could serve a more useful purpose with a modern building on it—these are factors in the vanishing of old landmarks.

Yet some are still around, often disguised by a new first floor decor fronting on the street. Others are in the least suspected places where only a trained eye will recognize them. Werner Lenggenhager has such an eye for detail and in his indefatigable wanderings back and forth across Washington with his camera he has captured the look of things here today that belong to the state's rich past.

BULL DURHAM was a familiar sign painted on buildings throughout the West. This is on the rear of a business block in Sprague.

ABOVE, SIGN IN COURT HOUSE, Davenport.

FRONTISPIECE, CLOCK ON 7TH STREET and Commercial Avenue, Anacortes. One of the very few with light globes.

# Contents

**ELEVATOR DOOR SCREEN, Mutual Life Building, Seattle.**

# False Fronts

HERE does one begin a sampling of what he has found? Perhaps the false fronts tell as well as anything about the past, whether it be in large or small communities. There are places in Washington that strongly resemble the frontier towns. Settlements began with high hopes, but not all grew and prospered. Once-thriving crossroads villages in some rural areas are almost deserted; in others business has picked up bodily and moved several miles away to up-to-date shopping centers.

Examination of sketches made between 1847 and 1857 in the Pacific Northwest reveals frame commercial buildings of severe lines. They were straight up and down, unadorned, with gable ends and plain ridge roofs. Quick construction and utilitarianism were the rule. A few of the more imposing that went up when haste was not imperative had slightly overhanging eaves and returned cornices, but merchants had another idea for giving the building deceptive proportions. Early in the 1850's the stark pioneer structures were interspersed with others that were small but had two-story-high fronts, some of them topped with sign boards that made them even taller.

Behind the square fronts were the same steeply pitched roofs and the rear gable looked as humble as its neighbors.

Such false fronts do not go back to the beginnings of our architecture, but are a style of construction purely American that moved across the country with the development of the West. It belongs to a time when streets were mud and sidewalks, if there were any, were of wood.

False fronts showed up in Washington settlements as soon as main streets became defined. They gave a citified look to the raw frontier towns, raising any shack to almost two story status and providing excellent space for advertising the various enterprises. Any owner could paint his name in big letters across the top of his premises and so gain eminence.

Those were days when lumber was cheap and charm was not an architectural accessory. If a town could claim this quality it generally was due to the scenic setting. Washington was bountifully endowed with picturesque landscapes that formed a backdrop for the glaring crudity of the board buildings. Weather and time mellowed them and in their decaying years they have been the frequent subject of nostalgic artists.

We accept the structures as having always been there, without pausing to reflect that they are only one step removed from the log cabins of pioneers. Almost as soon as there were sawmills and rough-sawn boards the false front was with us. Today who would waste high-cost lumber on such flimsy deception?

Scattered about the state, usually far from main highways, are towns that seem little changed since the pioneers were there. Service stations have replaced the for-hire stables, a strip of asphalt or macadam passes through, but most of the old buildings still stand, brightened by fresh paint or patent shingles.

Such a community is Anatone in the tableland 18 miles up hill out of Asotin. The town never incorporated. It has existed since 1878, when Daniel McIvor went there, built a log house and stocked a country store. His was the second place of business in the country. McIvor sold out that June, but his store survived and became the county's first post office.

The new owner, Charles Isecke, had to haul his merchandise almost 100 miles from Dayton. More settlers arrived and Anatone became the chief trading point of the surrounding ridges and the nearby

**LIKE ECHOES OF THE PAST are these buildings in Vader, Lewis County.**

METALINE FALLS.

portion of the Grand Ronde country. A blacksmith shop and Isecke's store were the main enterprises. A school started in 1878 in a log cabin. A sawmill in the area furnished the main payroll.

In its earliest years, during the Bannock and Piute wars in Oregon, the settlement had an Indian scare, entirely founded on rumor. It made such an impression that the people built a stockade, secured rifles and ammunition and spent several days inside the enclosure.

Another memory of pioneer days is of mail day on Saturdays when impromptu horse races used to be held down a quarter-mile stretch of the main street.

Anatone had a disastrous fire in 1896, but it rose again from the ashes much as one sees it today.

Metaline Falls in Pend Oreille County got its start with false fronts and that's the way much of it has remained. Minerals were discovered in the Metaline district about 1860 and placer claims were staked inside the townsite. Early miners thought the Pend Oreille River bed was strewn with gold. Lead discoveries caused a prospectors' rush in 1878. By 1880 the placer mining ended and the men went off to richer mines in Idaho. Permanent settlement began a few years later and the town was founded in 1909. Its big boost was from cement production, then it became a lead and zinc mining

center. The ore is shipped to Kellogg, Idaho for reduction. Mine tunnels run under the town; the cement quarry is on a hillside.

Langley, on Whidbey Island, was founded by Jacob Anthes, who when he moved there in 1880 found the south end of the island populated mainly by deer and large timber wolves. He spent his first winter hunting and fishing. During spring and summer four logging camps were cutting timber.

As population increased cordwood and water were to be had for tugboats at Langley. This was a

INDIANS AT NESPELEM copied the white men's architecture.

LANGLEY view north on Main Street.

sheltered harbor where they could pull in and wait for good weather.

Besides the cordwood business the few settlers cut brush, made it into bundles and shipped it to Seattle for rip rapping the city's waterfront.

Anthes filed on homestead adjoining Langley in 1886. When the Great Northern reached the coast in 1890 he sold Seattle's Judge J.W. Langley on the possibilities of a town. The latter incorporated the

Langley Land and Investment Co., which owned 700 acres with a mile of waterfront.

A storm wrecked the dock at Langley in 1894 and after that the steamers passed it up. Hard times followed. Most settlers left but Anthes stayed on. In 1898 cutting piling and brush revived somewhat and Langley started its slow comeback.

**FRESH PAINT AND A FANCY SIGN** brighten this old structure on Coupeville's waterfront. Several buildings near it were constructed a century ago.

**THE BOARD** walk in front of stores in Conconcully, Okanogan County, is like those of many years ago.

A FEED STORE opposite the Snoqualmie railroad station demonstrates good use of a false front for advertising.

POMEROY HAS FALSE FRONTS of brick. A central gable effect provides harmony and unity.

ORTING'S FALSE FRONTS have Mount Rainier for a backdrop.

THIS STORE AT TIGER, in the Pend Oreille Valley, has gasoline pump and "Coke" signs but not much else has changed.

OLD STORES in the 400 block on Wishkah Street, Aberdeen.

# Stores

COUNTRY stores had an essential role in the founding of Washington communities. It was a courageous man who moved west and staked his future on a stock of trade goods that represented his life savings. Or he might be indebted to a relative or friend for a grubstake investment in wares. The thing was to start with whatever would be in greatest demand. At first the appeal was to Indians who brought their harvest of pelts to the fur traders. This did not last long into the wagon-train period. Furs were hunted out, Indians were being pushed back and settlers were scattering over the land.

We aren't aware what stock Michael Simmons bought off a boat when he opened his store at Olympia about 1850. It may have been similar to that on the shelves of Charles C. Terry's emporium at Alki Point the following year. Terry's inventory included a box of tinware, a box of axes, a box of tobacco, a keg of brandy, a keg of whiskey, a box of raisins, 25 barrels of pork, 3,500 pounds of flour, 15 gallons of molasses, 800 pounds of hard bread, 400 pounds of sugar, some boots, shoes, cotton goods, glass windows and sash, grindstones, crosscut saws and files.

The kegs of whiskey and brandy were sure-fire bringers of trade. For years to come the only store in many a Washington community was also a saloon, with as much money passing over the improvised bar as was exchanged for merchandise.

The sole newspaper in Washington, The Columbian, in 1852 was characterized by its advertisements such as the one David Maynard ran for his store in Seattle. He announced that he was receiving ''direct from London and New York, via San Francisco a general assortment of drygoods, hardware, crockery, etc. suitable for the wants of immigrants now arriving.''

More explicit was the following announcement:
New Goods
Hourly expected to arrive per
Brig ''Jane''
Super superfine cloth coats
Super superfine doeskin pants
satinette pants
corduroy pants
Fine satin vests . . . . .
Tinware of every description
Sugar, tea, coffee, molasses, vinegar, pepper, allspice, nutmegs, saleratus, potash, soap, candles, tobacco

and a variety of other articles, all of which will be sold cheaper than goods have ever been sold in this place.

The same advertisement was run the next week and finally the third week appeared the words: ''The Jane has arrived.''

Only the seaport stores played up the names of ships. Inland merchants received their wares by more tedious means, at first pack trains and then wagon freight. Settlers east of the Cascades sometimes went to the store so seldom they bought calico by the bolt and sugar by the sack. Often their purchases had to last the family 10 to 12 months.

A woman in the Kittitas Valley recalled that her father would hitch up a four-horse team once a year and his wife and children accompanied him on a trip to The Dalles, Ore. to shop for food, spices, grain, candy, tools, seeds, muslins and calicos for everyday dresses and cashmere for Sunday-best clothing. It was an event long-anticipated through the monotonous months on the lonely farm.

**IN TROUT LAKE, on the south slope of Mount Adams, the store has a sheltered walk and a ramp for unloading freight.**

16

NIGHTHAWK OBJECTS to being known as a ghost town. Buildings like this may be old, but they are well painted and serve a farming district that has replaced the mines of past years.

Often produce was carried a great distance to the country merchant in the hope that it could be exchanged for needed items. Frequently the farm wife was destined to disappointment when the storekeeper declined to barter because he was overstocked with potatoes or onions or honey.

Not until automobiles and improved highways cut the distances between towns did the country store lose its eminence as a focal point in every community. Formerly the emporiums carried a general assortment of dry goods, farm tools, a little of everything that might conceivably be needed. There were no bakery counters, but there was plenty of baking powder, soda and seasonings. Spices were stored whole in a cabinet with many drawers. There'd be caraway seeds, hard round nutmegs, cinnamon stick and sarsaparilla.

Behind the counters were open bins filled with dried prunes, beans, sugar, dried apples and the like. Tin cannisters might hold coffee, tea and pearl tapioca. The coffee used to be sold unroasted, later it was roasted but not ground. The store would have a coffee mill for grinding the beans if a customer didn't possess a small mill of her own.

Glass cases were full of rock candy, jawbreakers, licorice whips, jelly beans, wafer candies with mottoes and mixed candy, especially the stick kind with flowers and stars in the center. Children made purchases with pennies that went farther than nickels do today.

There were no bottled soft drinks. Families made their own, such as root beer and raspberry shrub.

Stocks did not go out of date as fast as they do today. Staples in hardware, groceries and home fittings were the rule. Milk pans, kerosene laterns and crocks were common items. Thread was kept in a spool cabinet, dyes in another special cabinet. Nails were in kegs. Crackers were in open barrels

AT ALDERTON this store was modernized, but the false fronts show above the canopy. Erected in 1912, it was prettied with paint and flower baskets.

AT ELDON, Mason County the store has adapted to the needs of sportsmen and campers.

and gingersnaps in big round boxes. Bacon and ham were in chunks from which the storekeeper sliced the desired amount. Shoe buttons and buttonhooks were in regular demand. Cards of dress buttons were an important item. Lard was in tin buckets. Cheese was in round slabs, kept under an isinglass cover and cut with a huge knife.

Almost nothing was pre-packaged and before refrigeration perishables were few.

The country store was a general gathering place. It had its hitching posts or hitching rail out in front and sometimes it had a covered porch or space on the wooden sidewalk where in idle hours the proprietor and his friends sat, tipped back in armchairs. On rainy days these were pulled inside around the pot-bellied stove in the center of the establishment.

There are still country stores, but many of them on the inside are miniature super-markets. No longer does one enter them to buy tinware, stoves, paints, glass, plaster or buttons. More likely the casual visitor is seeking lunch meat for his picnic sandwiches, cola drinks or ice cream bars for refreshment on a hot day. The heavy shopping is done by car miles away in the chain stores. Something has gone out of rural living and it's a rare country merchant who continues to hold his own.

THE VINTAGE GAS PUMP in front of this old general store at Steilacoom indicates an effort to keep up with the times after automobiles came into use.

18

DOORWAY AT CROSBY AND MAIN Streets, Tekoa. The store has been in the family of William H. Dare since 1889.

THE POSTS AND COVERED WALK of this department store in Stevenson were typical of such establishments around the turn of the century.

THIS STORE AT DOTY may be dated, but the proprietor is on the ball with a frozen-foods counter and sports goods for passing fishermen and hunters.

# Blacksmiths

WHILE a store often became the nucleus of a town, sometimes a blacksmith shop appeared almost as soon. Years might go by with only these two places of business on the spot.

Occasionally a blacksmith shop was on a ranch and the owner's skills extended to repairing guns. A smith was much in demand and his patrons would arrive from many miles around, bringing their horses to have them shod. A product of such a ranch establishment was the branding iron, that long-handled accessory needed by the stockman to identify his cattle.

On the coast in an early newspaper L.H. Calkins of Olympia advertised: "Ship, gun and blacksmithing. Bring your wagons, carts, guns, ships, watches, clocks, etc. that want repairing." A competitor in the same city soon was announcing, "I have also commenced the manufacture of plows."

These versatile gentlemen easily branched into wagon making. Some expanded into selling farm, dairy and mill machinery. The humble blacksmith shop offered an unbounded future to an ambitious fellow.

After all, the blacksmith shop was the past equivalent of today's service station. Any horse was bound to throw a shoe at one time or another. If the community was small and the smith not very busy he farmed, tended a truck garden or did repairs. Kettle, coffee pots and kitchen equipment were mended in a blacksmith shop and it was the place where rims were put on wagon wheels.

If there was logging, a mill or construction going on broken tools needed repairing. Blacksmiths frequently made their own tools, particularly their hammers. Other articles of equipment were calipers, scale rule, chalk tongs, protractors, a sledge and the anvil.

They did almost anything with metal - bending, forging or welding. What put them out of business - besides the automobile - was electric welding, the acetylene torch and modern steel tools.

In the absence of a veterinarian they acted as horse doctor also. And on the Fourth of July, if no firecrackers were available sometimes the obliging blacksmith would provide a patriotic explosion for the festivities by placing gunpowder in a hole on top of an anvil, attaching a fuse and turning another anvil upside down over it. A bang of ample proportions resulted.

**MARY ANN CREEK, Okanogan Highlands. This shop in a mining district would have an ancient look were it not for the automobile tires in the doorway.**

**ENOUGH RIDERS frequent the beaches so that Nyberg's shop on Park Street, Ilwaco still shoes horses. The owner has been in business 44 years.**

AT ROY, John Napora graduated from mere horseshoeing into oxy-acetylene welding, cutting and brazing.

IN THE MEMORIAL PARK at Woodinville is this tribute to a village blacksmith, Johann P. Koch, born in Germany in 1877.

THE BLACKSMITH SHOP in the historical park at Cashmere was relocated from near Dryden. The log structure was built in 1889 by John Lanham and Leonidas Cutright.

WEEDS HAVE GROWN UP where horses once beat a path to the big door of the blacksmith shop in Moxee City.

THE BUILDING TO THE RIGHT used to bear a blacksmith's sign. Note the customary high doors to let a horse in. Granite Falls.

# Post Offices

SETTLEMENTS, no matter how small, had to have names and generally the postmaster presided at the christening. That is, he furnished the government with a suggestion and it was adopted unless there were too many others it duplicated. If he wasn't a sharp speller it was reflected in the end result, thus Whidbey Island was for years written without an "e" though Captain Vancouver's lieutenant, whom it honored, had one in his name.

Mail at first was picked up at Portland or San Francisco by anyone going in the direction of Puget Sound or Fort Vancouver, Walla Walla or Fort Colville. Magazines and papers were a rarity; only letters were posted. They did not travel in envelopes, but were sheets of paper, folded, perhaps tied with string, and always sealed with wax. The rates for a short distance in 1850 were 12 cents, and for a long distance 40 cents.

Early letters bore no postmarks. When envelopes began to be used, stamps appeared in place of the written cost of mailing.

A regular carrier was supposed to travel between Olympia and Vancouver once a month beginning in July, 1851. Many letters were lost or damaged on the way, as he had to ford streams and in bad weather was often delayed.

The first post offices in Washington were at Columbia City (Vancouver) in January, 1850, and at Nisqually. The latter was moved to Olympia by August of that year. Mail from the East arrived by way of Panama and San Francisco.

For nearly two years Seattle settlers sent a man by canoe to Olympia, paying him 25 cents for each letter. The first mail was not received at A.A. Denny's post office until August, 1853.

As late as 1880 mail went to Spokane Falls only once a week, carried on the back of a horse. Around the turn of the century in the rugged western part of the Olympic Peninsula a man earned $10 a month carrying the mail 20 miles to the Hoh, making three round trips a month requiring three days each. He considered himself lucky to have this income.

**ONCE A BANK occupied Hartline's post office building.**

Tales are told of the low esteem some postmasters had for their appointments. One Lewis County postmaster kept his mail and postal supplies under the bed. Another in Eastern Washington had it thrown loose in a trunk where patrons hunted their own letters. Before Lind had a post office a postal clerk would toss the mail sack off a passing train and the station operator placed it in a convient spot for settlers to help themselves. Similarly the mail was carried by steamboat up the Snohomish River in a sack left unlocked so that free access was had to it at way points.

Ritzville's post office, established in 1881, was at first in the pockets of William McKay, who besides being postmaster, was the county treasurer. He carried the mail with him, delivering letters whenever and wherever he met persons to whom they were addressed.

A man in a Benton County town was postmaster three years without an appointment. His predecessor abandoned the job as not worth keeping and the store proprietor told him to move out everything that looked like postal property and set up business in the railroad depot.

In towns everybody turned out to meet the mail when it was in. So often there was nothing for rural dwellers that they made no effort to get to the post office; therefore, the postmaster, who usually knew everyone's business for miles around, would try to send any important communication out by neighbors.

A few post offices became family institutions with several generations handing out the mail decade after decade. These long-term public servants and their families became authorities on local history and sources of much information about their communities.

Most postal service was handled with promptness after the state settled up, but an old resident of a Columbia River town, dependant upon boats said he could remember when the mail was tri-weekly —

try to make it the first week and make it the next!

Increased rural routes have caused scores of small post offices in this state to be discontinued. Changes are occurring constantly as the service is modernized and collections from mail boxes in such heavily populated places as King County now are taken to central distribution points. Thus the post-marks of communities that do have post offices are disappearing. A letter dropped into a box on the outskirts of Bellevue or Redmond may be post-marked Seattle.

The old-time functions of a post office remain intact at a distance from cities. Arrival of a certain truck or bus or airplane still may signify the hour for sorting the mail and be a magnet that draws citizens to peer in their boxes in the post office.

THE MODEST POST OFFICE
at Colton, Whitman County.

THE POST OFFICE, like other buildings in Trout Lake, seems to belong to a far-away past.

This is the rear view of what was SPRAGUE'S POST OFFICE until 1968. The new one is two doors away.

# Towns and Villages

AS population increased the professions and trades began to be represented and where there had been only a store, soon there was a village. The next step was platting and incorporation. And so towns came into being.

Most have been modernized to such an extent that they have lost their pioneer character. However, a few because of their striking natural surroundings or their remoteness from heavy traffic, have succeeded in hanging onto shreds of their past. Public spirited citizens and county historical societies have fostered appreciation of the heritage of some towns. In others it has simply proven good business to freshen up and preserve landmark buildings.

Seen from a distance, these communities create the illusion of remaining unchanged, but closer examination reveals the inevitable open spaces where buildings have succumbed to decay or the transformations wrought to accommodate new commercial enterprises.

Coupeville, Port Gamble and Port Townsend top the list of vintage towns. Skykomish is another. Poulsbo and Skamokawa retain some of their past character and the photographer has discovered bits of others that smack of old times.

The glowing promise of some was destined for unfulfillment. The first highly touted townsite in Washington does not exist on today's maps. It was Pacific City, a few minutes drive southwest of Ilwaco, promoted in 1850 and for two years thereafter. It was entirely a fake, though it did boast an uncompleted sawmill, a resort hotel and several cottages before the government took over the site for a military reservation and the occupants were ordered to evacuate.

The post office, Pacific City, survived longer than the townsite and for a time it was regarded as Washington's principal seaport. Dispatches in old files of San Francisco newspapers carried its dateline for several years after the scanty population had flitted or taken roots in Unity, later Ilwaco.

Another phantom city, Ocosta by the Sea, for a few glowing years was more than a plat on paper. Its promoters on Grays Harbor published a brochure telling how it would become a railroad terminus. Board sidewalks and streets were laid, a hotel was built, mills were started, but the bubble burst when it was realized that the site was completely unsuited for a deep-water harbor.

South Bend went through a similar railroad promotion period, when a rival townsite on the flats west along the river called Sea Haven, was boomed in 1889-90. Within a year it had a bank, newspaper, hotel and several other buildings. Here is how it was advertised in the puffball period:

"No deep draught sea vessels can get further up the Willapa River than Sea Haven . . . . It is the only townsite between the Golden Gate and Straits of Juan de Fuca where the largest vessels floating upon the blue waters of the Pacific can enter at will . . . It is only a question of time when she will rival San Francisco in importance."

County records showed the Sea Haven Land Co. proposed to build coal bunkers, docks, elevators, railroads, steamships and manufacturing plants. It was described as a million dollar corporation.

Eight years after Sea Haven's founding it was letting part of its lands out for hay and pasturage. Now one would have to hunt hard to find a trace of the burgeoning metropolis on a tideland ranch at Potter's Slough, although the platted streets remained on the tax rolls until about a score of years ago.

South Bend itself expanded in the same years, for the completion of a railroad was expected to mean great things. The town's population rose to 3,500, streets were planked and a large hotel was erected a few blocks from the depot. The hostelry never opened its doors.

Nevertheless the town thrived in the first decade of the present century and some of its large empty buildings are relics of that era.

Dream cities exist in county records elsewhere in Washington. The greatest dream of all was for a national city, which emerged later as Port Angeles. A reservation of 3,600 acres had been set aside in June, 1862 by executive order to be used for military, lighthouse, naval and other purposes, including headquarters of a port of entry. The following year 500 acres were withdrawn for a national city, which was divided into 803 town lots and acreage tracts. This was all done through the connivance of Collector of Customs Victor Smith, who had a personal promotional interest in the land and expected to profit richly from it. He was drowned at sea in 1865, his new customs house was carried out in a flash flood and the whole scheme fell through.

Port Angeles underwent another kind of boom in 1890 after the reservation was thrown open to settlement and the Puget Sound Cooperative Colony moved in. It was just before the great financial crash of 1893. Everybody was speculating in land, even to the extent of using the colony funds which had been paid in to purchase shares in the original enterprise.

Port Angeles then was typical of other little ports on Puget Sound. Its Front Street stretched two blocks long between bluff and beach. The sidewalks, a couple of planks wide, were on stilts several feet high to allow the tides to wash in and out.

Port Townsend was another city sharply divided by its bluff, but in this instance the split was into two strata of society. The bawdy seaport, with its sailors' boarding houses, its bars and "cribs," was frowned upon by primly respectable folk inhabiting the turreted and bay-windowed residences on the plateau 100 feet above the beach.

In spite of chain groceries, service stations and asphalt paving, Port Townsend retains an enviable character related to its glamorous past. Until the middle '80s it was a town of wooden buildings with only a few exceptions. In 1888 it had a population of 5,000 and its prosperity lay in restaurants, saloons, gambling houses, hotels and outfitting stores. It was distinctly a port of sailing ships.

When encroachment of steamships caused Port Townsend's marine business to fall off, the prospect of a railroad being constructed sparked a building boom. The brick structures on Water Street for the most part date from the late '80s and early '90s.

Some still were under construction when the great depression hit and the railroad work was halted. Banks failed and the new buildings went tenantless above street level. Carpenters were laid off and rooms remained unfinished for decades.

The buildings had relatively little use, and the clean atmosphere of the surroundings helped protect them from the ravages of decay. Thus they are remarkably well preserved.

**A ROW OF PIONEER BUILDINGS in South Bend has interesting roof lines.**

PORT TOWNSEND in profile. Note the bell tower.

There is nothing now on the waterfront to remind the visitor that this pleasant port by night used to be the scene of riotous living.

Dominating the rim of the cliff at Port Townsend are the venerable fire tower with its bell, St. Paul's Episcopal Church, the First United Presbyterian Church and several choice Victorian houses, two of them with mansard roofs.

Here and there other towns have changed little since their founding. For instance, Skykomish drowses beside the river of the same name, by-passed by the Stevens Pass Highway, on the opposite bank.

Platted in 1899 by John Maloney, the town was destroyed by a conflagration in 1904. Within a year buildings of better construction were erected and these were still standing until a recent fire. They included a four - story hotel, three saloons and a large billiard hall.

Maloney in early years owned a sawmill and after a time had a competitor, the Skykomish Lumber Co. But more important to the town's growth was its position as a division point for the Great Northern Railroad. Coal bunkers, freight yards and a roundhouse for helper engines supplied a rail-road payroll after construction days ended. Since the switch to diesel locomotives in 1956 the rail line has played a minor role in the town's life and

catering to sportsmen today is the principle source of income.

Poulsbo used to be called "a little bit of Norway on a fjord in Puget Sound." It is one of the most Scandinavian towns in the Pacific Northwest. Its main street looks modern but that is partly because a fire destroyed some of the older buildings that now are forgotten. Dominating the scene is the First Lutheran Church, located on a hill. The building, dating from 1908, replaces an older one erected in 1887.

Many of Poulsbo's inhabitants until recent years were fishermen. While some were connected with the Pacific Coast Codfish Co., which sent its boats annually to Bering Sea, others were salmon fisher-men who stored their craft at Ballard.

A notable feature of the community was its care of the orphaned and aged. It has had the Martha Mary Home since 1891 and the Ebenezer Home since 1909. (The children's home has twice been replaced.)

Poulsbo was named by I. B. Moe, first postmaster, for a spot near his home in Norway. It should have been Paulsbo, but the post office department erred and changed the spelling.

First comers to the area were loggers in the 1870s, followed by settlers in 1883, who arrived by rowboat. The shores were heavily timbered and the

LAKE STEVENS' old main street follows a winding stream.

fjord was called Dogfish Bay - now it's Liberty Bay. Dogfish used to be caught in traps and rendered into oil for greasing logging skid roads.

When the Spokane, Portland and Seattle Railroad was built down the Columbia, among the first towns to spring up was Bingen, laid out by P.J. Suksdorf in 1891 and named for Bingen on the Rhine. It became the shipping point for the western end of Klickitat County.

The post office was established in 1897 with Theodore Suksdorf as its first postmaster. Three lines of river steamers called but there was no railway until 1907. In 1910 the town had 200 population, a box factory, two hotels, two liveries, a general store, feed store, blacksmith shop, grocery, bakery, confectionery and newspaper.

The early industries were lumber, fruit growing

became the shipping point for the western end of Klickitat County.

The post office was established in 1897 with Theodore Suksdorf as its first postmaster. Three lines of river steamers called but there was no railway until 1907. In 1910 the town had 200 population, a box factory, two hotels, two liveries, a general store, feed store, blacksmith shop, grocery, bakery, confectionery and newspaper.

The early industries were lumber, fruit growing and dairying.

Lake Stevens was settled in the 1880's when Snohomish County was covered with virgin timber. Land clearing was tedious and there was no place for gardens until some of the forest could be cleared away. Cutting shingle bolts, logging and work on railroad construction provided income.

**COUPEVILLE'S MAIN STREET** backs on the waterfront at Penn Cove. The buildings are older than they look.

The townsite was platted in 1890 a mile away, where Old Hartford is. Another smaller townsite was platted along the lake shore near the Rucker Brothers mill. This was where the business portion of Lake Stevens eventually was built early in the present century. The first store was called the Lake Stevens Trading Post, taking its name from the scenic body of water two miles wide and three miles long. The Ruckers employed a physician and he had his office and drug store next to the mill. Next came a grocery, a meat market, barber shop, more doctors and another drug store, all strung out along the street bordering an artificial creek carrying the town's water supply. Down this street rolled the stage from Granite Falls to Hartford.

With construction of a new shopping center on Highway 1 A, much of the business moved away from the old main street, which now seems off the beaten track. However these buildings for the most part are still in use. The one in the center for many years housed the doctor, drug store and dentist. The pharmacy contained prescription records that went back to 1905.

Skamokawa at the mouth of Skamokawa Creek was dependent almost entirely upon water transportation and the stream was its main street. The winding east bank is lined to this day with structures dating back to the 1880's. Here were stores, hotels and wharves, connected by a continous stretch of plank walks. Sidewheel steamers and sternwheelers were daily vistors.

The old buildings are reminders of the days when families invariably owned a small boat for going to town with produce and to fetch the mail. The commercial center has moved to U.S. 830.

Skamokawa means "smoke over the water" for the fog that so often lay there. A local Indian chief also called himself by that name.

The town became known as a dairy center after William and Gus Prebstell opened a creamery. Several years later it was converted into the first farmers' cooperative creamery in Washington. Its building, erected in 1898, was adjacent to the present highway bridge. The creamery burned in 1947.

A venerable school house on the hill is now headquarters of Redman Lodge, Tribe 65. The building which formerly had a cupola was erected about 1896 on lower ground near the present bridge.

WINTHROP lies in a picturesque valley. Mount Gardner
is the snow-covered peak.

THE OLD PART OF SKAMOKAWA as viewed from the creek.

POULSBO is dominated by the First Lutheran Church on a hill.

BINGEN, named for a city on the Rhine.

SKYKOMISH'S old main
street.

THE HOTEL IN SKYKOMISH
features large covered
porches.

# Fences

ALMOST the first thing a settler did in new country after getting a shelter over his head was to build a fence to keep his livestock in and protect his plantings from stray animals. Where enough open prairie existed a pioneer might have a field ready for the sickle during his second year on the land. Invariably it was surrounded by a new rail fence split from fir poles, or from cedar, if there was a supply of this versatile wood handy.

All over this state one can find traces of the railsplitter's art, usually zigzagging through some mossy dell in a forsaken wooded corner of a ranch. What was once regarded as the easiest and most economical barrier to erect would today be considered the most wasteful. Trees were abundant then; they had to be cut down to clear the land and what better use could be made of them than to enclose one's fields? The snake or worm fence required no digging of post holes and no nails but it did consume a lot of rails. If not made of cedar it was also vulnerable to decay and many timbers would require replacement every ten years.

The customary process in Western Washington was to fell trees of a thickness that could be split twice into four rails. They were cut ten to twelve feet in length and, when sufficient were ready, they were laid along the boundary, one on top of the other, at angles so that they crisscrossed the ends of the next section of rails in the manner of log-cabin construction. This not only consumed wood,

but it took up much more land than the fences with rails inserted between pairs of upright posts connected with short braces. Much workmanship went into such fences, like the one **shown here** on old Highway 99 near the Napavine intersection.

There were variations of the rail fence, of which the most conspicuous was the horse-and-rider, with pairs of posts criss-crossed but not requiring to be dug into the hard ground. In some instances the crossed posts were surmounted by a third and longer one, the end of which touched the ground and was surmounted by another pair of crossed uprights.

In regions where wood was less abundant or had to be hauled a distance property owners made their rails go farther, designing fences in other ways which required less timber. As a consequence worm fences were seldom seen in some areas east of the Cascades. Instead the rails might be sawed fairly thin and nailed to the posts.

Rail splitting in those days was a regular occupation, with young men moving around and making a practice of hiring out to haul the timber, split it and fence new fields.

However these barriers were constructed, they were highly important because only if a farmer had a fence could he claim damage for trespass by livestock. Not only were cattle roaming at large, but bands of wild Indian ponies roved in open areas like Klickitat County.

In the 1880's ranchers of Eastern Washington demanded that the territorial legislature pass a law requiring stockmen to herd their cattle, so that it would not be necessary to build expensive fences to protect crops.

At least one man's fences long ago served a purpose for which they were not intended. The winter of 1889 was memorable for a terrible storm, which swept over the eastern half of the state. Settlers ran short of food and some had no means of keeping their families warm. A thrifty Lincoln County rancher pulled up his rail fences and sold them at five dollars a load to a neighbor for fuel, thereby

**ONE KIND OF HORSE-AND-RIDER** fence at Millersylvania State Park, Thurston County.

serving two purposes, rescuing a chilly family and restocking his own depleted pocketbook.

The shortage of fence materials east of the mountains was alleviated by the introduction of barbed wire, which was relatively cheap and had other uses as well. It was employed for emergency repairs of harness or farm machinery and occasionally provided telephone lines. The first one in the Palouse east of Colfax is said to have been completed by hooking up wire fences.

Earliest mention of barbed wire in Eastern Washington is in 1883. There was still the problem of erecting it in rocky terrain and where posts had to be hauled in. Here are some of the ways of bracing them.

Problems of fencing in the wheat country are non-existent today, for instead of farm animals, motor-driven vehicles and machines do the work. Grazing lands are turned to farms and wild horses are all but eliminated.

Still some picturesque fences survive, such as one at McAdams on the road between Washtucna and Palouse Falls. Lacking wood, the owner of the HU ranch used sod for his unusual enclosure for cattle. The few trees that grow in this area are only those planted around farm houses and these are far apart, due to the vast size of individual land holdings. The photographer was surprised to find that such fences sometimes were filled with manure.

A ROCK CRIB to support barbed wire near Cheney.

THIS RAMBLING SNAKE FENCE in the Pend Oreille country needed plenty of ground.

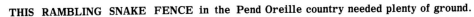

A SHEEP FENCE composed of two rows of wire netting filled between with manure, with barbed wire on top. One of the last of its kind, it is on the L. Jaussand ranch in Franklin County.

ANOTHER WAY TO CREATE A FENCE "POST" in difficult terrain. This is at Turnbull Migratory Water-fowl Refuge southeast of Cheney.

Sod-filled fence at McAdams.

PAIRS OF UPRIGHTS support rail fence in Lewis County. This is the Mary C. Miller farm at the Napavine intersection on the Jackson Highway.

PICKETS STAND AT COVINGTON like a line of worn-out soldiers reeling under the attack of an enemy — old age.

AN UNUSUAL GATE embellishes this rail fence at East Olympia.

# Schools

WITH the advent of settler's families the first thought was of schools for the children. The initial one was opened at Fort Vancouver by the Hudson's Bay Co. in November, 1832, with John Ball as teacher. His pupils were the offspring of company men who had taken Indian wives. There were also some children both of whose parents were Indian.

Other schools were founded in 1838 by Dr. Marcus Whitman and even earlier than that by Spokan Garry, an enlightened Indian chief.

One of the first for white children was in a log cabin erected by parents of 15 youngsters at Monticello (Longview). Olympia opened one on November 22, 1852, but it was a short duration, as on the night of December 26 the roof collapsed under a load of snow. Classes were continued in another building.

Whenever there were sufficient children in a neighborhood to justify it, parents attempted to arrange for some instruction a few months of the year. After the logs were cut for a tiny cabin there would be a group meeting to frame the building. Its equipment was primitive. The floor might be of split puncheons or hard-packed earth. The heat, if needed, was from a stick-and-mud fireplace. Water was from a dipper and a bucket carried from the nearest well. In a Thurston County district each child brought a bottle from home and when thirsty went to the corner where the containers were lined up on a bench and sipped from his own. Books were whatever the teacher could provide. Benches and tables were hand-made by the parents. Sometimes a bench was a split log with peg legs driven into it. The blackboard might be lengths of cedar fitted together and painted. A piece of sheepskin with the fur outside made an eraser. Sometimes there was not even that much.

Increasing population after a while necessitated better accomodations and little white school houses sprang up — they were seldom, if ever, red in Washington. First there had to be funds to build them. Money was raised in various ways. Donations were the rule, settlers giving labor and lumber. Ladies' committees raised cash from socials. Somebody would give a chair for the teacher. One school completely lacked chalk, so a carpenter donated a piece from his tool box until a supply could arrive.

A story is told of the first frame school at Puyallup in the 1870's. Railroad construction was in progress nearby and many boisterous customers rode into the Meeker store to make purchases. Ezra Meeker, angered by the rough language he heard on the premises, took a child's iron safe out of the stock and told his clerk, "I want you to see that every time anyone around here uses profanity he drops a quarter in the bank for the school as a penalty."

One day a strike occurred on the line and the superintendent riding out there, demanded of the foreman why the men were idle. On learning the cause he ordered that every blankety-blank one of them be fired. The story reached the small weekly newspaper and when the superintendent next visited the store he was told the rule. He dropped 25 cents in the bank and defiantly informed Meeker, "I will put in 25 cents every time you put in 50." Meeker took up the challenge and had to open the safe to get out more coins. When the contest ended the school fund was nearly $60 richer.

Some descriptions remain of other Pierce County

**LINCOLN COUNTY'S OLDEST SCHOOL, erected in 1879, has a place of honor in Davenport's city park.**

schools. A teacher said he was hired for $100 and board for four months, to begin any time he got there. Classes were held in an abandoned one-room house 12 feet square, standing in a fir clearing. A better school had been commenced but would not be finished for another year. At one place where the teacher boarded, the housewife, 16 years old, was among his pupils.

A teacher at the coal mine town of Franklin in 1874 held six months of classes in an unpainted rough lumber building, 35 by 45 feet, with a porch and anteroom. The school had three windows on each of two sides, a blackboard across one end and a raised platform for the instructor's desk, chair and an organ. A stove occupied the center of the building and a wood box stood in the ante room, which was also where the children hung their coats. This was quite a sophisticated outlay by early standards.

Any school with two rooms was considered big. A single-room building might house 50 pupils. There were no playgrounds and no gymnasiums. Multiple use was the rule. Not only were church and Sunday school held in the buildings, but literary and debating meetings, spelling matches and various sorts of community gatherings took place there. Elections invariably were held in them.

If the subscriptions promised for the teacher's salary failed to be paid, a school might close in six weeks.

"It was up to us to get as much from our schools as we could during the three months they usually ran," recalled a pioneer.

Men received better salaries than women, but the opportunity for selectivity was about nil and eccentrics often were the only choice, regardless of sex. One woman teacher in Pend Oreille County ended each day by taking out a corn cob pipe as soon as school was dismissed and lighting up. An elderly gentleman in the Cascade foothills had a bushy beard and a penchant for holding prayer meetings during recess or any time a pious crony visited the school. But the man could teach and his six pupils absorbed both learning and religion.

Applicants too young to rate a teaching certificate were given a special permit in some districts. Despite such alternatives, instructors were scarce and one woman in Kitsap County taught 13 months continuously, going to four different schools successively for 12-week terms. She covered all the schools in the county and that year there were no pupils in it that she didn't instruct.

Responsibilities were heaped on the young teacher. She was janitor and caretaker, usually beginning her day by starting a fire in the pot-bellied stove. If a snow storm came up, as they frequently did in Eastern Washington, getting the children

**SCHOOL WAS ORGANIZED AT HAVILLAH,** Okanogan County, in 1901 and moved into this log building two years later. Once 40 pupils attended classes here. The lean-to was added later.

home was her problem. Once this was achieved, school might take a three weeks vacation until the roads and trails were clear again.

Children of all ages attended these country schools. The older boys often indulged in chewing tobacco. By the time a lad was 14 or 15 he usually was needed on the farm and had to quit.

There was no coddling of the children and the whip or ruler, kept for punishing them, was legendary. But pupils remembered throughout their lives those teachers who succeeded in really teaching them something.

Before school and at noon and recess there were games such as hopscotch, black man, happy miller, ante over, one old cat, drop the handkerchief, pom pom pullaway, duck on a rock, run sheep run and blindman's buff. In very early days in Western Washington a few old log forts stood near the schools and the children used them in their play.

As late as 1947 Spokane County still had ten one-room schools within 20 minutes ride of the center of the city. One had a pump with a barrel in a corner and each child kept a drinking cup on a case nearby.

Only in extremely remote communities such as Stehekin, are one-room schools still in existence. If there is any means at all of getting pupils to a highway, a school bus or a car in which neighbors have gone together carries the children to a large union school. This applies to youngsters in such out-of-the-way spots as the Snake River Valley.

Union districts have resulted in abandonment of some large buildings like the one at Dungeness, now used for a community hall.

The forsaken schoolhouse at Ralston was in Adams County's last district to be consolidated. The community once had a bank, hotel, livery barn and other businesses and its population was 250 before the First World War. The children today are

sent by bus to Ritzville and their abandoned brick building standing in a wheat field is symbolic of what has happened to country schools.

Where Adams County once had 100 school districts it now has only five, one of them boasting the largest area of any in the state. A few pupils have gone as far as 45 miles to school each day; many of them travel 20 miles.

Visitors, seeing the well-equipped schools in Ritzville and its large garage for school buses, scarcely would associate the modern campus with the transportation problems which went with winter weather when children walked the snowy roads to their classes. Long-time residents remember a tragic day in 1950 when the district nearly lost a school bus and a dozen children in a blizzard.

Providence Academy in Vancouver, destined to become part of a community center and shopping area on the order of Ghirardelli Square in San Francisco, is the oldest school building in the state. By 1889 it was Washington's largest.

The first Providence Academy, 16 by 24 feet in size, was ready for occupancy in February, 1857. It began April 15 with seven pupils. In September the boarding school opened and later an orphanage. The present building was erected in 1873 and in 1889 an addition was built. The architect was Mother Joseph of the Sacred Heart, whose father was a noted architect of Montreal. She had helped him previously in his work. She was also the academy's founder.

**THE TWO-STORY BUILDING AT DUNGENESS is today a community hall and children from the district are bused to more modern facilities.**

THE FIRST SCHOOL AT EATONVILLE now stands behind the high school. For a time the structure, dating from 1892, was Girl Scout headquarters, but presently it is used as a store room.

Boarding schools like this in early days frequently received a pupil's tuition in the form of loads of potatoes, flour and beef on the hoof.

**THIS RED BRICK AT STEPTOE, Whitman County still does duty.**

PROVIDENCE ACADEMY,
Vancouver.

RALSTON'S LONESOME
SCHOOL, abandoned in a wheat
field.

SUPREME COURT JUSTICE
WILLIAM O. DOUGLAS attended classes here in 1904.
The building is at Cleveland,
Klickitat County.

THE DEEP CREEK SCHOOL
in Spokane County was used
until 1938.  It was built in
1880.

AT STEHEKIN Washington's only remaining one-room, log-cabin school still serves. It was built in 1922.

THE LOOP LOOP SCHOOL in Okanogan County is abandoned.

PIONEER SCHOOL in Walla Walla's historical park.

# Churches

AFTER taking care of the pioneer's temporal wants the next concern was for matters of the spirit. Religion entered Washington with the establishing of Hudson's Bay Co. posts. Upon completion of Fort Vancouver in 1825 Dr. John McLoughlin continued the custom begun at Fort George (Astoria) of holding Sunday services. For Church of England followers he read from the Book of Common Prayer and for the Catholic company servants he held a service in French.

The Rev. Herbert Beaver was stationed at the fort between 1836 and 1838 and conducted the first regular Church of England services in the officers' dining room.

The initial Catholic mass offered north of the Columbia River was at Fort Vancouver in 1838. That year Fathers Modeste Demers and Francis N. Blanchet arrived to begin the Catholic missions which sprang up in both Eastern and Western Washington.

Meanwhile Dr. Marcus Whitman had reached Waillatpu, close to Walla Walla, in 1836 and founded a station for the American Board of Missions.

Another early church was begun for the Indians by Spokan Garry, who had been indoctrinated in the Church of England faith. His tule-mat structure on the bank of the Spokane River may not have looked like a house of worship but it predated most others in the state.

Other denominations came later. The Rev. John P. Richmond was briefly at Nisqually in 1840. The first Methodist service was held in Olympia in 1852 in a saloon on Main Street. A cannon was fired to announce the event.

Several restored structures remain east of the Cascades as relics of the early period. Among them is St. Michael's Mission, recently relocated from northeast of Spokane to the campus of Fort Wright College on the edge of the city.

The original mission was founded in 1866 by Father Joseph M. Cataldo, superior in charge of all Jesuit establishments in the Northwest, who made it his headquarters.

Some of the state's most venerable houses of worship are in Port Townsend, Port Gamble and Steilacoom, but there are others, particularly in small communities that rival them in picturesqueness. Usually these early churches ran to Gothic style with an occasional touch of whimsy in their decoration.

Few look their age as thoroughly as the one in Tacoma's Old Town. The congregation was organized on October 30, 1884 by the Rev. John F. DeVore, builder of an earlier Methodist Church at Steilacoom in 1853. It is said that at that time he went to the owner of an Olympia sawmill and asked for a donation of lumber. Because of his Sunday-go-to-meeting attire, the miller thought the minister obviously was not about to engage in heavy labor. Devore, said the miller, might have what lumber he could carry to the Sound in one day. This suited the reverend gentleman very well. An athletic man, he appeared at dawn, worked until sunset and carried off enough boards to build both a church and parsonage.

Tacoma's Old Town Church was enlarged in 1889 and retained its steeple-like arrangement of a bell on the top of a tall stump, still a landmark. DeVore never was in charge of the completed church; its first pastor was the Rev. G.A. Langdon.

The classic concept of a country church is Christ Lutheran at Egypt in northern Lincoln County, not far from Old Fort Spokane. It was built in 1906 after services had been held in a schoolhouse for a number of years.

The congregation was founded in December, 1890 and the parsonage was erected in 1892. Early pastors also served Reardan and Davenport, traveling by livery team or bicycle. It was only in 1911 that services in the English language began; prior to that they had been in German.

In 1957 the church was turned around to face the highway and enlarged Sunday school facilities were added in the new basement. Two years later a new constitution was adopted, replacing the original, written in German. Many descendants of the several founding families are still members of the church.

Years ago the ringing of church bells on Sunday morning brought out the majority of the population. There was no golf nor any television to distract

ST. MICHAEL'S MISSION.

them from worship. Besides that, the church-going element predominated in most counties.

The first preaching in new towns was generally at the home of the pioneer minister. Then donations of labor, materials and funds resulted in a building, much in the manner of raising a school. If the community didn't as yet justify a church, the school-house sufficed and a visiting minister from another district dropped by for occasional preaching.

Camp meetings were another development which presented an excuse for the people from some distance roundabout to get together.

At Satus, the Indian church, now abandoned, was patterned after those of the white man but was devoted to the Shaker religion, a hybrid faith, combined of medicine-doctor rituals, Protestantism and Catholicism. The usual scene of worship was an oblong wooden building with benches placed around it. In front was an altar with lighted candles, crosses, sacred pictures and two bells. Before the service was ended each worshiper shook hands with every person present. The Indians moved in a procession around the floor and some

of the leaders would seem overcome by tremors or shaking spells.

Another Indian church, the first on the Colville Reservation, was erected at White Stone, but was moved two miles south of Nespelem when waters of Lake Roosevelt threatened to inundate it.

Mary Queen of Heaven Church in Sprague was built in 1902 at a cost of $10,000 and was described at the time as an ornament to the city. It has a natural finish wood interior, white and gold altars and colored windows.

The parish is one of the oldest in the diocese of Spokane and in its first years was shepherded by visiting Jesuits who went there on horseback. Services began in 1882 in a small rough building, with the Rev. J. Joset, S.J. presiding. He had come down from Spokane Falls to open the Catholic house of worship. So many persons attended that the structure would not hold all of them. It was decided at once to erect a better church, so one went up the next year and by 1885 there was a resident priest. In 1887, the same year the town's Catholic Academy, St. Joseph's, was built, the church was

**THE LOG STEEPLE** of Tacoma's Old Town Church.
enlarged. Still this did not suffice and at length the ornate Mary Queen of Heaven Church was erected.

Wilkeson had a community of foreign miners, reminders of which are its Holy Trinity Orthodox Church and Slovenian Hall, erected circa 1910. The latter was the fraternal and social center for 1500 miners and families.

The exotic steeple on Zion Congregational Church in Ritzville has a foreign air that is the heritage of its builders from their Eastern European background.

In 1883 a party of 17 Russian-German families arrived at Ritzville by wagon train from Nebraska and brought to an end a long series of moves. Their ancestors had migrated from Germany to Russia in 1765 after the Seven Years War and lived on the Volga steppes more than 100 years before changes in conditions sent them to the New World. Empress Catherine the Great had offered the emigrants tax exemptions for 30 years, free choice of land, free transportation, government loans and no requirement of military service. Gradually her bill of rights was overridden and the soil, as well, became exhausted. Economic and other considerations sent the Germans to the New World and they moved to Nebraska around 1876. Dry seasons influenced them to again seek new homes and thus the first party ventured to Ritzville. They filed on land, scattered and wrote to relatives that the country was good and to come. The colony multiplied in hundreds and Russo-Germans became the dominant population group in the Ritzville area.

They organized a German church as soon as the first ones arrived and meetings were held in homes. In 1890 a church was built four and one-half miles west of Ritzville. Eventually there were both German Lutheran and German Congregational Churches in the town itself.

St. Mary's Mission for the Indians was established on the bank of Omak Creek in Okanogan County by Father Etienne DeRouge in 1886. A boarding school for boys was opened and in 1905 a day school for girls. These attained college level in 1909. A hospital was added to the mission the next year.

The church, erected in 1905, is the oldest building there today. The main altar was built by the combined efforts of the Indians and some of the valley settlers.

St. Mary's is the only boarding school for Indians remaining in Washington.

CHRIST LUTHERAN at Egypt, Lincoln County.

STEEPLE of a former Methodist Church built in 1870
at Tumwater. It is now a Unitarian Meeting House.

**UPPER LEFT:**

UNIQUE IS THE COMMUNITY CHURCH at Cedonia, Stevens County, built in the 1890's and still used for Sunday school. When seen directly from the front it looks like half a church, sliced down the center, with an out-size steeple perched at one side.

**UPPER RIGHT:**

LUTHERAN CHURCH at Havillah, viewed from the school house.

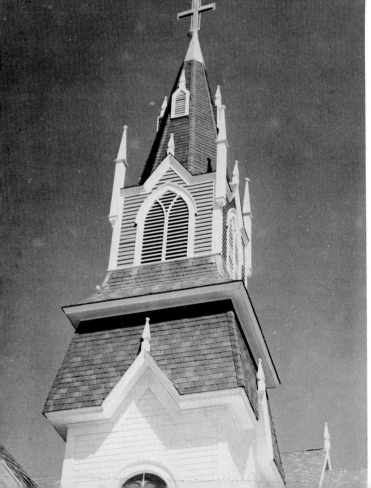

POULSBO'S distinctive steeple.

INDIAN CHURCH at Satus.

INTERIOR of the church at Satus reflects Shaker customs.

MARY QUEEN of Heaven Church, Sprague

THE BUILDER of this church on the Colville Reservation was Chief Skolaskin, prophet and medicine man.

**HOLY TRINITY Orthodox Church, Wilkeson.**

**ZION Congregational Church, Ritzville.**

**PEACEFUL SCENE beside a Columbia River slough in a Scandinavian community on Puget Island, Wahkiakum County.**

INTERIOR of church, St. Mary's Mission.

FIRST Baptist Church, Olympia.

GENERAL VIEW of St. Mary's Mission in Okanogan County.

# Mining Towns

EARLY in Washington's history another kind of town sprang into existence with the discovery of mineral deposits. First to develop was Bellingham, where coal mines were worked along the shore of that port city beginning in 1852.

The first gold find to be publicized in Washington was near Fort Colville in 1855.

Soon afterward a gold rush developed in British Columbia's Fraser River Valley and the argonauts, hastening in that direction in 1859, found more of the precious mineral along a border stream, the Similkameen River. At one time it was estimated 3,000 men were at work from the falls of the Similkameen to where it empties into the Okanogan River.

Prospecting south from British Columbia in the early '60s, miners discovered placer deposits at Ruby Creek in Whatcom County, the Sultan basin in Snohomish County, and the Swauk and Blewett districts at the Kittitas-Chelan County line.

Because part of the mineral belt in the Okanogan was inside an Indian reservation created for Chief Moses in 1879 these areas did not reopen to prospectors until the executive order was withdrawn in 1890, after the chief's people moved to the Colville. When restrictions no longer limited settlement, miners thronged to the border region and a host of lively communities sprang up along the northern rim of the state.

Nighthawk began in 1899 with a mine, general store and post office. The Nighthawk mine was on the east wall of the Similkameen River valley a few hundred yards from the post office. A 20-stamp mill was near the east portal of the main tunnel. Another company was south of this mine and the Six Eagles group was one mile south of Nighthawk. Others were not far away — more than 30 mining enterprises between there and Loomis.

The veins were especially developed around Nighthawk, Golden and on Palmer Mountain. The principal mining was along the Similkameen halfway between Oroville and Nighthawk, where over $500,000 was extracted a short time after the discovery.

The mineral belt extended south of Nighthawk through Okanogan County to Conconully and Ruby and on west into the mountains around Harts Pass. Mining began around Loomis in 1891 and a five-stamp mill went up, the first in the region. Its success opened the way for at least eight other stamp mills.

A contemporary wrote, "Here you will find miners who have been in every mining camp in the known world, from the burning sands of Africa and

NIGHTHAWK has many scattered old buildings.

52

WHAT'S LEFT of the Ruby silver mine at Nighthawk.

Australia to the Yukon River in Alaska and the Andes Mountains in South America. Canada, Mexico and Spain are represented, as well as all the camps in the United States. The 49'er can be found here too in all his glory. But with all this motley throng there is less lawlessness than in many Eastern cities.''

The town of Loomis began as a winter cattle station in the early '70s. J.A. Loomis, pioneer merchant, arrived in 1886 and his ranch was the main business place in the country. Loomis operated it jointly with Guy Waring and they engaged in the selling of general merchandise throughout the mining excitement.

At its peak the little town in a ravine had a main street three blocks long, strung with eight saloons, two dance halls and three general stores. Beds in those days were at a premium.

No one knows how old the mysterious 10-foot arrastra at Blewett is or who used it. The depression, shaped like a Mexican hat, is an attraction at this ruined mining camp in the Cascades. There is a belief that Indians took out gold there and dragged stones over ore in the crude mill.

After returning Cariboo miners discovered the rich deposit large mining interests set up a three-stamp mill, powered by a water wheel. Later a larger mill of 20 stamps was built about 1891. Mining continued until the Alaska gold rush, when the men deserted for what they supposed was a richer field. A few stayed on and in the Depression were joined by others, panning Swauk Creek to feed their families.

One of the richest mines in the Blewett district reportedly was dynamited years ago by miners incensed over cancellation of their lease on the property.

A post office was established at Blewett in 1893 and named after Ed Blewett. The town then consisted of a hotel, saloon and 13 cabins.

In 1886 glowing reports of silver mines in the Okanogan caused Charles Ballard, a civil and mining engineer for the Northern Pacific, to set up an assay office under a pine tree and lay out the towns of Conconully and Ruby. The first discovery in the Salmon River area was at Ruby Hill that same year. Quartz lode mines already had been found near Conconully as early as 1871. At one time 1,000 miners were in the vicinity.

The town was called Salmon City in the first two years of its existence, then the name was changed to Conconully, an Indian word meaning ''evil spirit,'' applied to a mythical monster in the adjacent lake.

A fire in 1892 laid two business blocks in ashes. The story is told that several kegs of beer were rolled out of a saloon during the conflagration, but they were not saved. Some of the crowd breeched them and got too drunk to be unhappy about the blaze.

Another disaster was in store for the town two years later when snow melting in the mountains swelled the tiny Salmon River into a torrent. It was on a May morning in 1894 and the inhabitants all had advance warning, so were able to reach high ground in safety. The water spread 12 feet deep in the town and destroyed 42 buildings.

The final blow to Conconully was a drop in the price of silver. The miners drifted away and near-by Ruby became a ghost town, of which almost no trace remains.

The gold rush to Ferry County began in 1897; the land was opened to mineral location the following year. By 1899 Republic and Keller were wide-open gold mining camps with a few shacks and log cabins, but mostly the men lived in tents or in the open. The first stores in both towns started in tents, with supplies brought by pack horse over Indian trails. Republic was originally called Eureka.

In 1889 to get to Index one had to travel by boat to Snohomish and from there by smaller boats to Startup and by pack train the rest of the way. A hotel went up to accommodate miners, bound for Silverton, Galena and Monte Cristo, and surveyors who were working for the railroad then due to go through Stevens Pass.

By 1891 rich strikes of gold, silver, copper and

lead ore had been reported in the mountains, the railroad construction was approaching and the hotel enlarged. It had no running water in the rooms and each had its wash bowl and pitcher to be cleaned and refilled every morning. Kerosene lamps also required cleaning and filling. Every day was wash day, with sheets, pillow cases, towels and table linen rubbed by hand on the wash board.

By 1893 the town's population was 500, with 800 to 1,000 prospectors and railroad men coming and going. A tent hospital was established and a school.

In summer of 1893 fire, started by a man reading in bed with a candle, destroyed almost the whole of Index.

By then the railroad had been built and the mining excitement had died down, but in 1897-8 it resumed with development of Sunset copper mine. Two new hotels, a drug store and other shops were built and a newspaper was established.

Ore from the region went out to the Everett smelter.

Not far southeast of Seattle are remains of active coal mining at such places as Bayne and Black Diamond.

The high point of the coal industry was reached in 1917 and 1918. Then it began to taper off until now the black mineral cannot compete with Diesel oil and electricity. Coal's days as a fuel seem to be over, unless it is to supply power.

Black Diamond was on the western edge of the Green River coalfield, where the mineral was discovered in 1880. It was the type desired for locomotives and steamships and some was so clean it needed no washing.

Every coal mine at the turn of the century was adjacent to a close-knit little community of miners, many of them of European origin. Italians, Poles and Slavs dominated the industry's labor supply. Families continued to live on in the area long after the tunnels were blocked and railroads quit running to the coal fields.

Roslyn has preserved its identity as a coal town through the years, though its population is not what it was at the peak of its mining career. The black mineral was known to be in the region as early as 1881 but it was two years later before "coal float" was discovered. Claims were staked along the well defined veins and by the end of 1886 a branch railroad reached the town and was carrying out carloads from the new coal field. By 1901 it was producing more than a million tons a year.

The miners who settled there were Scotch, English, Welsh, Irish, Slovaks, Italians and Poles, who preserved some of their folk customs. Roslyn always was a colorful place in spite of the great dismal heaps of black slag and the black mouths of its tunnels.

**STONE STORE building at Loomis.**

REMAINS of stamp mill at Blewett.

CONCONULLY and its lake.

REPUBLIC has a flavor of the past, but it still is a producing mining center.

THE TOWN of Index with Mount Index in the background. Houses have steeply gabled roofs because of winter's snow.

ASSAY OFFICES are relics of Washington's gold rushes. This one at Molson is owned by the Okanogan County Historical Society and has been turned into a museum of mining relics.

INSIDE is a portable oven used for testing mineral samples. Lying on top of it is an old-time miner's cap with lamp.

CHESAW has numerous buildings remaining from its years as a mining center. One suspects that this structure may have been a saloon. Apparently it serves now for a summer home.

THIS ASSAY OFFICE at Chesaw was built in 1900 by the first assayer in Okanogan County.

THE TIDY LOG assay office in Cashmere's Mission Park pioneer village was brought from its original location at Blewett Pass and reassembled. It dates from 1879.

THREE FAMILIES still live in the old mining town of Bayne, King County. The car at left once brought coal from the mines.

A MOUNTAIN of slag at Black Diamond.

REMNANTS of the former business district of Black Diamond.

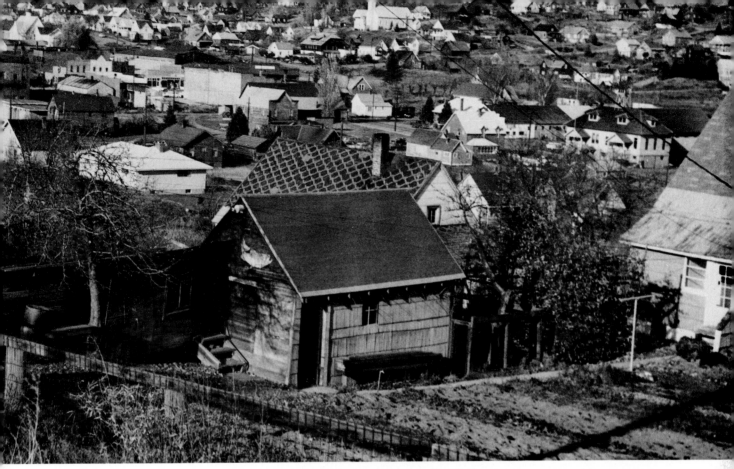

GENERAL VIEW of Roslyn, where coal is still king.

STREET SCENE in Roslyn. It has changed its appearance little with the passing years.

# Industries

WASHINGTON'S first industries were grist mills and sawmills started by the Hudson's Bay Co. before fur trading went out as a prime source of income. Salmon salting, horticulture and the raising of cattle for hides also were initiated while the company still was in its ascendancy.

The Americans brought in other industries - tanneries, brick kilns, lime kilns, shingle-cutting - but there was not really much variety. Men worked mostly as loggers or farmers - frequently both.

Logging with oxen netted earnings before anything else, for San Francisco, in need of piling and timbers to replace damage from repeated fires, sent vessels to carry these products away. The few sawmills cut lumber for local consumption. Settlers preferred board houses to those of logs, if they could get them.

Pioneer mills consisted of upright "muley" saws driven by water power. Their output of planks was not always uniformly straight.

Such mills have vanished, as have the ox teams and skid roads. Sawmills themselves went through different phases, from the great band saws for slicing through forest giants to today's smaller saws for second-growth timber.

Grist mills likewise disappeared from the scene. Ten miles out of Woodland is the Cedar Creek mill, erected in 1876, the restoration of which is a project of the Fort Vancouver Historical Society. It leases the structure for $1 a year from the Washington State Department of Fisheries. The latter bought the property in order to improve the salmon run in the stream. A dam which fed the flume leading to the mill's water wheel was torn out and a fishway was built. This left the mill without water and useless. It was threatened with ultimate collapse when the historical society went to the rescue.

The first American flour mill in the Inland Empire was built in 1859 by Judge B.F. Yantis on Little Pend Oreille River in the Colville Valley. His original plan was to build on the Spokane River and trade with the Indians, but Spokan Garry broke the agreement.

The mill was a log house, 12 by 14 feet, put together with wooden pins. The grinding stones were less than 10 inches across and set to run vertically. Water flowed over a makeshift dam and turned a water wheel. The flour was sifted through a cloth as it left the stones.

Yantis sold the mill in 1861 and the later owners improved it, adding a set of French burrs in 1863. They built an addition, employed a miller and he in turn made a set of millstones of native granite and added cleaning machinery so that a good grade of flour could be made. The mill was torn down in 1918.

Most conspicuous reminder of the time when flour mills sprang up in the wheat country is a building that dominates Waitsburg and was once its largest industry. This is the Preston-Shaffer mill, started in May, 1865 by Sylvester Wait, founder of the town that for a time was known as Wait's Mill. The first set of stones, brought around Cape Horn in a sailing vessel, was still in use 70 years later to grind coarse grades of flour.

When Wait built the farmers agreed to hold their grain for him until spring and save themselves the trouble of hauling it to Walla Walla. Wait bought his machinery on credit in San Francisco and it was delivered that winter. Lumber was so scarce that an old sheep corral and other structures were purchased in order to obtain boards.

Wait sold his mill to the Preston brothers in 1870. It changed owners several times and was greatly enlarged until by 1881 it was producing 450 barrels daily. That was the year the Oregon Railroad and Navigation line reached the town. In 1900 seven flour mills were operating along the Touchet River in a stretch of less that 30 miles in the vicinity of Waitsburg.

With the flour mills there was need for storage of the grain before it moved out by rail.

The first steel wheat tank in Washington was built at Ritzville in 1901. It was 40 feet in diameter and 50 feet high and held 55,000 bushels of grain. It stood beside the Ritzville Flouring Mills.

Throughout the wheat country in that period it was customary to see near railroads great stacks of burlap grain bags reaching the height of a two

MILLSTONE AT ELLSWORTH, Clark County, where there was once a grist mill. Similar stones can be seen at Vancouver, Seattle, Colville, Waitsburg and several other places in the state.

story building. The sacks were piled solidly and sometimes planks were laid on top like a gable-ended roof, with the bags filling up all the space to the ridge. Other times the sacks were piled like an annex to a warehouse, making it look double its size.

A symbol of changing times is the salmon cannery. Where the Columbia River used to be lined with them - the number on the Oregon and Washington sides together reached 39 in the early 1880's - only five are left on the Washington bank. Except for two, these are small custom establishments for putting up fish caught by sportsmen.

The passing of canneries has been gradual. Most of the Columbia catch now is taken to Oregon to be canned or is sold on the fresh market. Much the same thing has happened in the Puget Sound area. Fish are still caught in quantities off the San Juan Islands but canneries no longer operate there and the catch goes to Seattle or other Sound ports.

On the Columbia long ago it was supposed the supply of fish was inexhaustible. Salting of salmon was begun in 1830 by the Hudson's Bay Co. and

this method overlapped into the canning period, which commenced in 1866 at Eagle Cliff, Wahkiakum County. The peak of the industry was reached in the 1880's and continued until the 1940's. So many companies competing for salmon drove the price up and the heavy fishing caused the runs slowly to decline. In the industry's infancy 200 cases was considered a good day's pack for a cannery, but with improved methods this figure rose to 4,000 in the large establishments.

With the decreased supply and restrictions shortening the fishing season, the canneries for the most part fell into disuse. Built over the water, often in exposed positions, they succumbed to weathering and little remains of many except for rows of piling out in the stream.

Altoona, down river from Skamokawa, had the last surviving cannery in Wahkiakum County. The Columbia River Packers Association operated it and at one time it was the largest in the county. In 1945 it was converted so as to can tuna also.

The cannery at Ellsworth, Clark County is used at present to store fishermen's boats and during the buying season salmon are loaded there, packed in ice for transport to Astoria for canning.

The building dates from 1917 and was erected by the Columbia River Packers Association. On one of its peak days it put up 142 tons of fish. At that time there was no eight-hour day and the cannery operated May through November each year. In 1943 canning was discontinued and since then the building has served as a buying station.

A thriving industry of long ago which left peculiar souvenirs was the production of coking coal at Wilkeson, Pierce County. The ovens extended for a distance of several blocks along the edge of the town, but traces of them are vanishing as gardeners and builders carry away the bricks for home use. Stripping has gone on for years until the once-conspicuous structures are easily passed by unless one is looking for them.

These ovens were built in 1888, the first on the Pacific Coast. Their purpose was experimental. There were 25 at first, then 50 more in 1891. By 1925 Wilkeson had 160 ovens in operation. At Wilkeson and nearby Fairfax 400 men were at work for the Wilkeson Coal and Coke Co. The town was named for Samuel Wilkeson, a director of the Northern Pacific.

The ovens are alongside a rusty railroad track in a bank with brick-lined and formerly rock-faced caverns. The bank is overgrown with trees.

Wilkeson had and still has another old industry, the cutting of sandstone for building materials.

Mysterious towers of the past are several crumbling lime kilns in the San Juan Islands, reminders that the white stone once was an inducement to settlement of parts of the archipelago. Burning of lime commercially began about 1860 in crude pot kilns. A little later they were improved and another kind, remaining at what was the Eureka quarry on San Juan Island, took their place. Ultimately there was a more modern installation at Roche Harbor and a thriving industry centered at that place.

The towers were filled from the top with wheelbarrowloads of rock. Fire was set under it by means of the opening, which was then sealed. After several days of burning and cooling, the white mineral was removed through the same door. The lime was packed in barrels and shipped to the mainland for mortar and fertilizer and in later years for use in manufacturing paper, sugar and other products.

The big deposits were worked out and became uneconomical to operate. There are still lens and

**CEDAR CREEK MILL, 10 miles out of Woodland.**

pockets of limestone in the islands, but not enough to justify development of cement works, the quantity market for limestone today.

Martin Schmieg, the first brewer in Washington, just had started at Vancouver when the Fraser River gold rush began and he followed the crowd as far as Steilacoom in 1858. Three years later he sold out and moved to Seattle, where he joined Amos Brown in erecting a brewery at First Avenue and Columbia Street.

The Capital Brewery was established at Tumwater in 1896 by Leopold F. Schmidt of Deer Lodge, Mont. and Louis Schmidt of Butte. They put up their brewery and ice plant where a tannery had stood.

Raising of hops went with the making of beer. It was the most sensational boom industry to hit the Puyallup Valley soon after its settlement more than a century ago. Success of the undertaking caused the hop farms to extend out through Issaquah and up the Snoqualmie Valley to North Bend and in the Stillaguamish Valley from Florence to Arlington.

James R. Wood, owner of a small brewery in Olympia, finding it exceedingly expensive to bring in hops, imported some roots from England and tried them in his own garden. They grew well and he sent a few in 1866 to John Meeker, at Steilacoom. The latter took them to the Puyallup Valley, where his father, Jacob, and his brother, Ezra, had homesteads.

The plants thrived and the first year of their harvest of catkins (dried in a loft over their fireplace) the Meekers sold 185 pounds in Olympia at 85 cents a pound, more money than the average settler could expect from all his crops in a season.

What followed partook of the aspect of a gold rush. Pioneers plowed their acres, eager to try this crop. The Meekers were not averse to selling the roots. Ezra Meeker soon became known as the hop king and went to London to study aspects of cultivation and to act as agent for the growers in the Western Washington Valleys.

There never was a question what a new settler would plant in the Puyallup whether he cleared one acre or 50. Each September hordes of Indian pickers arrived to harvest the hops, which were placed in large boxes having handles at the sides. The Indians were paid by the box.

Hop picking was an annual event, looked forward to with pleasure and calculation of profit. Everybody who could for miles around helped in some way with caring for the crop. Some pulled up poles for the pickers, others drove teams hauling the boxes to the kilns or took care of the curing and pressing.

At first drying the hops necessitated experimentation. It was found that a heated drying floor and sulphur to bleach the catkins and prevent fermentation were not enough. The hop houses had to have openings at the sides and top to let out steam. The ideal kiln was a square two-story building

with a cone-shaped roof. The wagon might enter the second story, where the hops were dumped onto drying racks. Here they had to be turned over frequently.

A large flat-topped stove on the lower floor kept the heat at the right degree. The sulphur was placed on top of this stove.

When the hops were thoroughly dry and ready for baling they were put into presses and came out covered with burlap. These were stacked, ready for shipping for making of yeast and beer and for export.

Had it not been for the Indian labor there probably would have been less profit for the farmers. The Indians made a big affair of hop picking, arriving by horseback, wagon and canoe. They brought their dogs and their families, from babies to crippled grandmothers. At night drum pounding, gambling games and wailing kept up a constant din in the Indian camps. The tribesmen fished and dried salmon on racks over smoke pits, watched by some ancient squaw weaving a basket.

The hop industry flourished despite efforts of the temperance organizations to check it. What they couldn't do a tiny insect accomplished. In the summer of 1892 Puyallup Valley farmers noticed their vines had a faded look. Massed on the under side of each cluster of leaves were scores of hop lice. Simultaneously Ezra Meeker received letters from other hop-growing regions on the Pacific Coast, all speaking of the infestation and asking for help.

A spray that had been tried in England was introduced, but did not prove entirely successful, as it was costly to apply and damaged the vines.

Other methods were attempted, but the quality of the hops deteriorated until the pods were a scant third of normal size and the growers were forced to give up. The hop yards were plowed under and the farmers turned to other crops.

This was not completely the end. A solution to the louse problem was found and, after repeal of Prohibition, hop growing was resumed between 1932 and 1950.

Hand-picking was necessary with hops grown in Western Washington and they could not compete with those machine-picked in Central Washington.

The market also has changed and fewer hops are used in American beer.

So today none are grown in the Puyallup Valley. You can still find there some of the splendid homes hop fortunes built and, in the fields are the picturesque kilns, sometimes surrounded in spring by glorious acres of blooms raised by the bulb growers who farm the same tracts.

In the Snoqualmie Valley at Fall City is a hop shed dating from the 1880's. The shed formerly stood by the river but has been moved several times. It was put together of morticed six-inch timbers and hand-made nails.

In the heyday of hops as many as 2,500 persons,

both whites and Indians, moved into the Upper Snoqualmie country for the picking season. Sundays they would stage horse races at which much betting was done especially by the Indians.

As we have said, logging was just about the state's first occupation, especially on Puget Sound.

Nothing remains of the industry as it once was, except for tools and photographs in historical museums. In a few places perhaps it is possible to find the remains of skid roads or at least the scars left by them. The last logging railroad has ceased operation and the only survival of past years is a lone flume, having its terminus at Underwood, Skamania County. Many like it used to be found between 1900 and 1935. In 1953 four still survived in the Pacific Northwest, but today only this solitary timber flume exists in the United States.

It was the longest one for lumber ever built. Constructed in 1923, it cost $10,000 a mile, but it proved very economical to operate, as almost no manpower was involved.

The flume carries boards from the Broughton Lumber Co. sawmill at Willard to the planing mill at Underwood, nine miles away. Lumber drops in the swift-moving stream and is not touched again until guided onto rollers at the planing mill. The last 100 yards is level, to allow the boards to slow down.

Sometimes there is excitement and danger when one of the trestles clogs and men have to go out with poles on the narrow and usually slippery walk over a canyon to clear the passage.

HOP DRYER at Alderton, Pierce County. Poles still stand in the hop yard.

OLD BREWERY at Tumwater.

THE "GRAVEYARD" of a hop dryer at McMillin.

HOPS WERE ONCE BIG BUSINESS at this Orting farm where bulbs now are grown in quantities. The drying shed was a double-ender.

HOP BOXES on Mrs. Mary Geiger's farm at McMillin.

THIS CLOSE-UP of the hop dryer on Mrs. Geiger's farm shows details of contruction. The hops were unloaded on the upper floor and the fires were down below.

THE PIONEER HOP SHED at Fall City for which a permanent home is sought.

BROUGHTON LUMBER CO. flume, nine miles long.

ANOTHER VIEW of the same flume near Underwood, the longest for lumber ever built.

ONE OF THE ROW of coking ovens at Wilkeson. All are so overgrown they are difficult to distinguish, especially since quantities of bricks have been carried away from them.

THIS TOWER was once a busy lime kiln at Eureka, San Juan Island.

THE ALTOONA cannery on
the lower Columbia River.

GRAIN ELEVATORS of all sorts dot the wheat country.
This oldtimer at Touchet has its mouth open, ready
for the arrival of a load by truck. Formerly the
grain was hauled in by teams.

# Banks

ITH industries soon there had to be banks. The first in the Pacific Northwest opened in Portland on June 1, 1859. Soon afterward Washington got one – after a fashion – in a coffee barrel in Dexter Horton's general merchandise store in Seattle. Horton had started in the business with Arthur Denny and David Phillips, but when the latter two were elected to the territorial legislature they sold out to their partner. He took his interest on credit.

As an accomodation to customers he cared for their valuables, hiding them in the coffee barrel and elsewhere about the store. The money sacks increased, most of them derived from logging, and Horton saw that he'd have to find a more secure depository. In 1870 he was in San Francisco buying for his store and before leaving purchased a second-hand safe.

With Phillips he organized a bank, dividing his store in half to accomodate it. For the next ten years it was the only financial house in the city.

Meanwhile Walla Walla actually was ahead of Seattle and banking in Washington officially began there in July, 1869 with the opening of the A. H. Reynolds Bank. It was followed in November of that year by the Baker-Boyer National Bank in the same city. Then came Phillips, Horton & Co. in June, 1870.

This company built the first real bank structure in Seattle in 1875, a one-story stone building 28 by 70 feet in size. It had three arches across the front, two over the windows and one above the entrance, giving it considerable dignity amid the pioneer shacks.

Old bank buildings, now devoted to other uses, can be identified because of their look of stability, in harmony with the character of the institution. Everywhere in pioneer towns the bank stood out among the rest of the business places.

Banks had to be strong buildings to protect their deposits and so these structures have survived long after their owners were gone. Most often they were located at the corner of a block and the ornate doorways are a clue to their original use.

An item in an 1890 booster book reflects the feeling about banks. Telling about one to be erected in Bucoda, the editor observed, "It is safe to predict it will be the chief architectural feature of the town.

Spokane's first bank represents a combination of early industry and trade that evolved into a financial operation, much as did that of Dexter Horton.

In 1871 two men settled at Spokane Falls and installed a muley saw, run by an overshot water wheel. It could produce 700 feet of pine lumber in a day of hard work. Two years later James N. Glover bought out the pioneer lumber men and brought in a better mill from Salem, Oregon. It had a five-foot saw and a four-foot edger and proved entirely too large for the meager amount of business available. When Glover found his venture unprofitable he opened a trading post, exchanging cheap blankets, shawls, calico, beads, tobacco, knives, sugar, tea, coffee, groceries and red face paint with the Indians for furs, particularly marten. He did very well until the pelts within 100 miles or more of the falls were cleaned out. Trade became so poor Glover closed shop. He sold his operation to A. M. Cannon in 1878 and the latter had the courage to hang out a sign: "Bank of Spokane Falls – A. M. Cannon."

He admitted he lacked money, but his sister-in-law had $1,000 and promised to loan it to him. With the Northern Pacific building westward, he believed he soon would have pay checks to cash and that he ought to be ready. His venture paid off. Cannon's was the first bank east of the Columbia and north of the Snake River.

Washington's oldest national bank charter was issued in 1876 to the First National Bank of Walla Walla, of which Levi Ankeny was president.

In 1889 there were 51 banks in the territory, but with acquisition of statehood the number jumped to 114 within the year. Until then no bank in Washington had failed, but the record was broken in 1891 as a result of the demise of the great international banking house of Baring Brothers and the near-panic which followed.

Bankers had many humorous stories to tell of finance in early times. For example, when Adams County was organized the newly-appointed treasurer was informed there was some money at Colfax, the old county seat, of which he must become custodian. Not expecting any great sum, he was startled when he was paid $700 in gold.

"I never saw so much specie in all my life," he said later. "They put it into my hands and told me to clear out. In those days we did not have banks and safety-deposit vaults and there I was with that gold to take care of. I just took it home and hid it in the bed. I tell you it was a white elephant to me until we spent it."

Levi Ankeny once related a tale about Sam Lichtenstadter, a merchant at the gold-rush town of Ruby who became something of a financial acrobat. In order to save the cost of transporting money the 160 miles between there and Spokane he worked out a plan to save his community the heavy discount for carriage.

"He began," Ankeny related, "by establishing his place of final redemption at a Spokane bank, through which he transacted his mercantile business. Then he ordered several thousand artistically lithographed checks – pink paper – made payable in Spokane to bearer, meantime having put in a safe and the conventional country cage and hoisted the sign of The Bank of Ruby.

"The system he was about to carry into effect may be readily understood. To all depositors and on all exchanges or credits he issued his personal check against his own credit in faraway Spokane. The sign having been swung prematurely – that is to say, before the pretty pink checks arrived – a man named Keene appeared with a huge gold nugget as big as one's hand, in exchange for which he desired to get $250 in money. But the young banker had not enough bills or coin to cover the value of the nugget and in this predicament he told Keene, as a reason why he could not accommodate him, that the Bank of Ruby was a bank of deposit only."

"At this critical point in the unique career of the Bank of Ruby, when the blossoming scheme was threatened with the blight of scandal, when there was danger of a run against it before it had secured a depositor, a mining operator who was going into the mountains for a few weeks walked in and confided to the young banker's keeping a goodly sum of cash. After he had left Lichtenstadter explained to Keene that he was only joshing him and meant all the time to help him out with the cash, which he did and took

**THE SMALL WHITE BUILDING** with three arches across the front, in Uniontown, Whitman County, was a standard design for pioneer banks.

the nugget. Next day the bundle of pink checks arrived by stage and the bank was saved.''

Ankeny added that the bank issued nearly $300,000 in checks payable at Spokane, where few of them found their way. They passed as currency throughout Okanogan County and as far north as Penticton and were acceptable even to the county government. The first oddity that surprised the visitor was the omnipresent pink check.

A mine buyer once appeared with a $10,000 draft he wanted cashed. Lichtenstadter wanted a 5 per cent discount. The holder said he didn't propose to be robbed outrageously. The banker said that was what it cost to bring cash into the country, but if the man liked he would issue his personal checks against the draft in any fractional amounts the man desired and they would serve just as well as gold.

The holder wouldn't listen to such a proposition, but everywhere he went he saw the pink checks moving freely and finally was convinced they were the money of final redemption of the camp and exchanged his draft for a pocketfull of them.

Failure of the Spokane National Bank and collapse of the Okanogan mining boom caused the downfall of the Bank of Ruby, which redeemed every pink check that could be drummed up. In the last analysis $3,000 worth had evaporated.

Banking equipment in territorial Washington generally included a gold scale to weigh dust or nuggets of miners passing through.

There was a tendency in many towns of old families to stay with the banking business. They were conservative to begin with. At the first Washington bankers' convention in 1889 one opposed the ''bad practice'' of paying interest on deposits. The session frowned on a proposal for a mutual arrangement so that banks might draw drafts on other banks for the convenience of the public. This later became common, but it was too revolutionary for that day.

**THE OLD NATIONAL BANK at Spring and Main Streets, Colfax.**

INTERIOR OF THE Molson State Bank in the pioneer village at that place.

THIS KIRKLAND BUILDING with corner entrance was intended for a bank by the town founders but was never used as such.

ANOTHER CORNER BANK. This one at Oakville is at present an antique shop.

RAISED SIDEWALK in front of the old bank of Silvana was intended to protect pedestrians from flood water.

THE FIRST NATIONAL BANK of Conway now affords a comfortable private home for one of the town's residents.

MEMORIES of the days when no town seemed too small to have its bank.

# Hotels

HOW could any area grow without a hotel? It had to have a place for newcomers and their families to stay in those first nights before they found land of their own or before the husband went to his new job. Then there were the loners who required room and board regularly.

Washington's first newspaper displayed an awareness of the hotelman's trade. In volume 1 number 1 of The Columbian appeared this announcement:

Cowlitz Hotel

A Great Desideratum!

The subscribers have retitled and greatly improved their House at Cowlitz Landing and are now prepared to accommodate the public with the best the country affords.

Saddle Horses

can at all times be had upon reasonable terms.

(In case you didn't know, "desideratum" is "that which is desired.")

The same paper of the fall of 1852 carried this notice:

Olympia House

corner Main and Second Streets.

The undersigned having opened this House of public entertainment for the accommodation of the traveling public, he will furnish man and beast with the best fare the market affords. His table will at all times be supplied with fresh fish such as Salmon, Halibut, Trout, Mackarel, Cod, Herring, Flounder, Pilchard, Crayfish, etc. etc. Also with fresh

Oysters, Lobsters, Clams, Bear, Venison, Pheasant, Grouse, Rabbit, Partridge and Quail, together with the finest Oregon Beef, Mutton and Pork also the finest desserts of Cranberries, Whortleberries, Raspberries, Blackberries and, in short, Olillies of every kind; all got up by an accomplished Chinese cook who comes highly recommended by the American consul at Canton.

Olympia being the point where the main road from the Columbia River strikes the Sound, pleasure parties and others wishing to go down the Sound will find this the best point to start from, as suitable boats for that purpose can be furnished at reasonable rates.

Private rooms furnished to those wishing them.

Edmond Sylvester.

**DACRES HOTEL in Walla Walla was built where the Stine House had stood. The metal balcony was a distinguishing feature.**

FRIDAY HARBOR'S Tourists Hotel has seen better days. It once had a porch across the entire front.

Unlike Sylvester's arrangement, more often the cook in the pioneer hotel was the wife of the owner. A few energetic women set up hostelries, such as Seattle's Madame Damnable and Olympia's Aunt Becky Howard, who kept the Pacific House. This hotel was opened in 1854 by William Cock and in February the first session of the territorial legislature met there. Pictures of the building show it to have been two and a half stories high with a false front, 12-paned windows and trees growing around the corner lot on which it stood.

A few years later Mrs. Rebecca Howard took over the management. She was a Negro and a former slave. Both she and her husband were excellent cooks. Mrs. Howard became corpulent and wealthy and on her death left a considerable fortune to an adopted half-Indian boy. During her tenure at the hotel she educated and supported the orphaned daughter of her former master in the East.

Mrs. Howard still was in business when President Rutherford B. Hayes visited the territory in the fall of 1880 and he was entertained at her hostelry. Its dining room often was the scene of merrymakings during legislative sessions.

Two years later the Carlton opened and by 1890 had become Olympia's leading hotel. It was three stories high, the top floor having a mansard roof. A porch ran across the front of the building, which could accommodate 90 guests. It advertised

"commodious sample rooms, a gentlemanly clerk, a reading and writing room."

Another rival establishment was Youngs Hotel, formerly the Washington. It boasted a bar, billiard and pool tables. The bar was important, for, as someone in Olympia wrote, "Legislation without irrigation is stale and unprofitable work."

Finally there arose the big Olympia Hotel, which stood on the present post office site until a fire destroyed it in 1904 after 15 years operation.

Bagley's history credits David Mauree with running the first public house in Seattle. He opened a dining room in Dr. David Maynard's residence early in 1853 and soon afterward moved across the street, where he furnished lodgings in a loft.

A more complete and comfortable establishment was opened a little later by Mary Ann Boyer, a native of Pennsylvania, who became Mrs. Conkling. In 1860 she was still single, aged 58, and her net worth was $3,000 — quite a sum in those days. She had a well built two-story house at the southeast corner of Main and First Avenue S., which stood until the fire of 1889. The place, called the Felker House, was one of the conspicuous structures on the early waterfront and one map points it out as "Madame Damnable's."

Mary Ann earned her nickname from her coarse loud voice and tendency to profanity, which she demonstrated when on October 22, 1854 the district court convened at the Felker House. At the conclusion the proprietress submitted her bill for the use of her best room for the session, $10 for rooms for the jurors, $4 for furniture and 50 cents each for jurors' meals.

'Tis said that the prosecuting attorney, feeling the cost of meals was high, asked for a receipt for them.

Mary Ann Boyer could neither read nor write and was so incensed at this request that she ran to the kitchen, grabbed sticks of fire wood and threw them at the attorney. He fled without the receipt.

Mary Ann's husband was an old sea captain, who until his marriage was noted for his strong vocabulary. His wife however could outswear him and he became a mild and inoffensive mate by comparison. Like many a rough woman of her day, the hotelkeeper was noted for her tender heart, therefore was remembered with mixed sentiments long after the hostelry was gone.

In the triangular block where Yesler Way and James Street join at Pioneer Place stood the Occidental, run by John Collins. He had started in the hotel business by becoming manager of Pope & Talbot's Teekalet Hotel in Port Gamble. In 1867 he bought a third interest in the Occidental, moved to Seattle and almost at once purchased another third. By 1882 he was sole owner.

When President Hayes arrived in Seattle this hostelry was the scene of a banquet in his honor.

As soon as Collins was in entire control of the

Occidental he razed the wooden building and replaced it with another of stuccoed brick, having a mansard roof and bay windows framed in ornate cast-iron moldings. It was the most elegant hotel north of San Francisco.

During the Chinese riots a gang stormed into the building to tell Collins they had come for his Orientals. He replied that he'd shoot the first man who laid a finger on his Chinese. The intruders threatened to return and said he'd be sorry. When they had gone Collins rounded up his pig-tailed crew and locked them in the cellar of his house across the street, stationing an armed man on guard. Not one rioter showed up.

When the great fire of 1889 swept around the Occidental it wasn't lost without a battle. Collins had his Chinese on the roof with wet blankets beating out the showers of sparks. By the time the conflagration reached Marion Street the wooden planking in both First and Second Streets was burning. Collins tried to buy the wooden houses across James Street from the Occidental to dynamite them for a fire break, but the owners would not sell. An hour later they were burning. The heat broke the Occidental's windows and it burst into flames.

Collins went deeply in debt in order to rebuild. Then came the financial collapse of 1892-3 and he was losing so heavily on his many investments he turned the new hotel into an office building, renting rooms to dentists, lawyers, dressmakers, anyone who could pay a few dollars. A bank moved into what had been the lobby. Collins managed to hang on and the Alaska gold rush saved the building for him. He was able to turn it back to its former use, though he renamed it the Seattle Hotel. It remained the city's leading inn until the Washington, or Denny, opened in 1903. Even after that it continued to have a great following. The building was a landmark at the triangular corner and some years ago efforts would have been made to save it, had there not been earthquake damage which caused the cornice to be removed and otherwise downgraded the structure. In 1960 the hotel ceased to exist and made way for a parking lot.

Another of Seattle's grand old hotels was the Butler at Second and James. Here the "best" people congregated. The dining room was divided in the middle by graceful arches separating the men's and women's sections. At dinner time a well remembered Greek musician, Nicholas Oeconomacos, held forth with an orchestra, playing soft music in the old tradition.

Walla Walla in 1873 claimed the largest brick hostelry in Washington Territory. It was the three-story Stine House, on the site where Fred Stine built a small shanty in 1862 and commenced

a lucrative blacksmithing and wagon-making business. Stine never owned the hotel, but it carried his name.

Brick for the building was made in Weston, Oregon, and hauled in by wagon. The lime was from San Francisco and cost $80 a barrel delivered. The window glass was from France by way of Cape Horn.

The hotel opened in August with a grand ball. The greatest event recorded in the establishment's history was a dinner given President Hayes and party. The menu was printed on white satin with a gold border and the dishes were listed in French – slightly misspelled.

A bridal chamber was a feature of the hotel and may have accounted for the many weddings held in the building. In the early '70s it was headquarters for the stage lines to Lewiston and LaGrande. In winter the coaches drawn by six horses each were a great sight as they raced down the street to deposit passengers.

Two fires damaged the hotel, the second one in the early '90s leaving it in ruins. The owner sold to James Dacres, who in 1900 opened the 78-room Dacres Hotel on the same corner. The building had a metal balcony around the second floor and out in front it was lined with potted

MANSARD ROOFS were great space savers for early hotels. This brick stands in Palouse, Whitman County. Formerly it must have had a porch surrounding the main entrance.

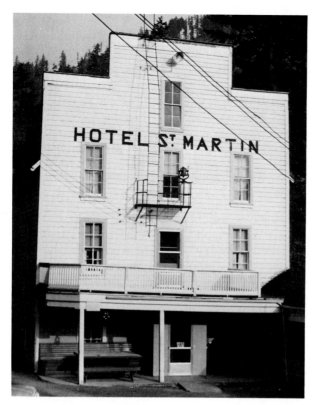

THE HOTEL St. Martin at Carson is a rare survivor among mineral spring resorts.

VACATIONERS ENJOY prowling around Roche Harbor's venerable Hotel de Haro where President Theodore Roosevelt once was a guest.

palms. Stages no longer ran, but Dacres provided a horse-drawn vehicle that met all the passenger trains. Among his distinguished clientele were John Philip Sousa, Louisa May Alcott, Al Jolson, Harry Lauder and President William Howard Taft.

Spokane's first hotel was the Western, where bear skins and buffalo hides were laid on the floor for beds. It cost 50 cents a night to stay there. A ladder was the way to the second floor. A horse doctor was the host.

Patrons were cowboys and miners, who enjoyed washing and bathing in a half barrel of water in which floated a bar of soap. Staple foods were bear, venison and salmon.

The next hotel was the California House, with eight rooms on the second floor and above them an undivided loft, known as the corral. A double bed was in each of its corners and here men could bring their blankets when the other rooms were full.

This hotel meant as much to the community as the Davenport does today. Parties and dances were held in it, with music by one or two fiddlers. Presiding in the kitchen was a Chinese cook, who occasionally got drunk. Then townswomen had to be summoned hastily to help out.

Good food was an important asset in the business. New Tacoma had a hotel at the wharf that always served dinner shortly after arrival of the train. A prelude to it was half a dozen steamed clams,

so delicious that often patrons called for a second helping.

A good many hotels got their start during railroad construction, when a small country place might feed as many as 80 men. Any community where men congregated, such as the miners at Blewett and the oystermen at Oysterville, necessitated accommodations. Usually some housewife was ready to provide meals and lodgings for them. The cost might be 25 cents a meal. In fact an 1881 advertisement for a three-story fireproof brick spoke of board $5 a week and with room $6 a week. At Montesano a free bus met the trains and top prices for everything were $1 a day.

Announcements emphasized the family dining room, parlor looking on the busiest street, accommodations for commercial men, theatrical people and transient guests, special rates for regular boarders. Gamages Hotel at Hoquiam claimed to be "more like a home than a public house." It boasted "none but white cooks" (in other words, no Orientals) and "courteous and attentive lady waiters."

In 1890 Bucoda was claiming a hotel "built in a substantial manner with hard finish throughout and illuminated by electric light." Centralia's Park hotel had "wires laid to every room to furnish the incandescent lights that will be in operation shortly." It had a billiard room and "hot and cold water baths at hand." Another hotel had everything for the "festive commercial traveler."

Seattle, more sophisticated, had gas at an early date and guests were confronted with signs in their rooms, "Don't blow out the gas." Anyone who failed to turn it off might not wake up.

In 1891 Patrick Welsh opened the Tourists Hotel in Friday Harbor and exactly ten years later absorbed his competitor, the Bay View Hotel in the next block. He converted it into the Tourists' Annex. A bar and a pool room contributed toward making the hotel a rowdy spot and when the Sunday closing of saloons went into effect in April, 1905 the event was celebrated by patrons who bought up a quantity of liquor on Saturday night, then held a burlesque religious service in the bar room the following day.

It was alleged that gambling also went on in the hotel saloon after a man was stabbed there in a fight over a pedro game. Presumably there had to be some place in the sleepy island town where fishermen and quarrymen could find a little excitement on a weekend.

The Hotel de Haro once took care of employees of the Roche Harbor Lime Co. and guests of the firm. Among notable names on the register is that of Theodore Roosevelt, who made a cruise to the San Juan Islands during his presidency. Members of the hotel staff point out a place on the second floor where ancient timbers are exposed. The impression prevails that these are part of a Hudson's Bay building, but the company never was involved in anything more than running sheep at this end of the island. Probably the log structure dates from settlers who went there in the 1870's.

Outlook Inn on Orcas Island is much older than it appears to be. Charles W. Shattuck built a log house at Eastsound in the 1860's and it became the hub of island activities, as he added a store and post office. Above the store was a dance hall.

Shattuck and his family lived at the rear of the building until he sold out in 1887 to Walter Sutherland, a New Yorker. Sutherland added more rooms and turned the rambling structure into the East Sound House. The village had in the meantime become one of the most desirable summer resorts in the Puget Sound country.

It is said that Shattuck's original building to this day forms a part of the hotel.

Back in 1910 Washtucna aspired to become the seat of government for a county that never was formed. Today it is barely inside the southern boundary of Adams County.

The town, of less than 350 population, lies in the bend of a coulee where the cross-state highway from Seattle to Pullman crosses the Ritzville-Lyons Ferry route. The name of the place is a mystery. It is reputed to have been so called for an Indian chief of long ago. Three clear springs of soft water, flowing seemingly from solid rock, made it a winter retreat of Indians who grazed bands of ponies on the high bunch grass.

The surrounding country was a treeless waste when in 1878 George W. Bassett settled there. Four years later Washtucna became a post office, the mail arriving in pack sacks on horses. Until letters were called for they were held in an old trunk belonging to Mrs. Bassett.

The region was a stockmen's paradise before homesteaders drifted in and discovered that high-grade wheat could be raised on Rattlesnake Flat, five miles north of town. Soon wheat growing took over on three sides of Washtucna, where formerly there had been only wild horses and range cattle. A grain elevator was built in 1891, after the Oregon Improvement Co. constructed a rail line from Connell through the Washtucna Valley to Moscow, Idaho. The route became a

TRULY A country hotel is this inn at Washtucna.

PART OF Outlook Inn at Eastsound dates back to the 1860's.

CHELAN was laid out in 1889 and the Hotel Chelan was built in 1901. The town had a military post in 1880 but it lasted only a year.

branch of the Union Pacific and the town was a rail junction point.

The town's population has varied little in the present century. Trees planted three score or more years ago are taller, the once-rutted and dusty main street has been surfaced and service stations replace the "fine livery accommodations" advertised in 1908.

Washington's mineral waters and hot springs formerly were economic assets, attracting health-seekers for leisurely vacations. Today thermal cures no longer are in fashion and what they once accomplished is now achieved with pills and prescriptions. People have no time for leisurely dips and sips at a spa and the unhurried life which characterized them has almost disappeared.

St. Martin's at Carson is one of those which has survived longest. In 1910 there were two others in the vicinity, Shepherd's on Wind River and Collins', two miles away on the Columbia, while at Mineral Springs, 14 miles up the valley, another resort was erected. Some of these retreats were open summer and winter, with coaches meeting trains and river boats.

St. Martin's spring was discovered in 1876 by the children of Isidor St. Martin, who one day were sitting on a log by the river with their feet dangling in the water and found the stream at that point was warm, not cold. The property was railroad land, but later the father was able to homestead it. In 1900 he built a shelter and gave mineral baths in wooden tubs.

While St. Martin's still operates, the hotels at Collins, Shepherd's and Government Springs are dismantled. Collins began in 1900 with five tubs, later being enlarged by 16 more tubs. Added attractions were riding horses and special launch transportation. When business fell off the hotel and bath house were torn down. Shepherd's, a three-story hotel and bath house, burned in 1930. The Government Mineral Springs Hotel, built in 1909, burned in 1937. Visitors still camp on the grounds and drink the soda water.

### THE NIGHTHAWK HOTEL

T. C. VAN EATON'S original log cabin is part of the hotel at Eatonville. See right hand corner of first floor.

THE OLD lobby of Randle's Hotel is now a store.

THE CAPTAIN Whidbey Inn on Whidbey Island is a log structure erected in 1907.

THIS PART OF the Bennett Block, built in Spokane in 1890, is the Adlon Hotel.

# Lodges

SOCIABILITY was part of the pioneer scene and men missed the opportunity to fraternize. Historians seem to have ignored the lodges that sprang up in the West, but the newspapers very early carried notices of their activities and meetings.

Free Masonry is the oldest of the fraternal organizations in the Pacific Northwest, beginning in 1846 when steps were taken to obtain a charter for a lodge in Oregon City.

The first one in Washington was organized in Olympia in 1852 and chartered the following June. Within another six years there were three others north of the Columbia – at Vancouver, Steilacoom and Grand Mound.

Olympia lodge Independent Order of Oddfellows received its charter April 10, 1855. By 1873 there were 54 lodges of the order in Oregon and Washington Territory.

An 1869 account tells of the Olympia group purchasing a site for an ''elegant and spacious'' hall. The building was to be of two stories, the first floor occupied by several business offices and a school room. The second floor had the lodge hall and a library. About the same time the organization established its own burial ground.

Another bit of lodge news was recorded in Olympia in 1866 when 30 or more ''staid and law-abiding'' citizens assembled at the Methodist Church to form the Independent Order of Good Templars, thus ''inaugurating the first organized effort to stay the ravages of intemperance.''

In Port Townsend this lodge was laughingly referred to as an order of reformed drunkards, some of whom did not remain on the wagon any great period of time.

A similar fraternal organization was the Order of Champions of the Red Cross, formed in Olympia in 1872. It purchased a building in 1877 and, in spite of being low on funds, got it carpeted, neatly furnished and supplied with an organ.

''Its members,'' said an announcement, ''are bound together by mutual obligations to protect each other against intemperance and vice and to exercise among themselves the principles of charity and brotherly love. Its objects are to shield the innocent, to succor the tempted, to encourage the the struggling, to bury the dead, and more fully to strengthen the bonds which should unite all true men and women in their mission of mercy and love.''

Other lodges have come into existence since, but these were the ones on the pioneer scene. The old Masonic and Oddfellows halls still stand in many a rural community.

**ODDFELLOWS Hall in Orting.**

RED MEN'S Hall in Ska-
mokawa stands on a hill. It
was once a school house.

ALTHOUGH BUILT in 1903, this hall is still in use.
Note that the Oddfellows left their chain on the front.

THIS STRUCTURE has served many purposes. Besides being the Roy Theatre, it was its Oddfellows Hall and now is a tavern.

PORT GAMBLE has the second oldest Masonic Hall in the state, built in 1876.

ODDFELLOWS HALL in Issaquah was typical of many small town lodges. It has the ever-present three-linked chain in front.

THE MASONIC Temple at Olympia was built in 1910 on the site of an earlier building.

ELLENSBURG'S Masonic Temple has an exceptionally ornate decoration on its upper floor.

THIS Oddfellows Hall in Port Townsend dates from 1897, but an imaginative paint job has completely transformed it.

# Court Houses

FORMATION of a county seldom was the excuse for plunging into the expense of providing a costly seat of government. It often began with rough quarters where the auditor might keep his records. Initial expenses were for a chair and table and the books – in earliest days with pale blue pages – on which he entered minutes of commissioners' meetings, sales of property, charges for the care of prisoners and expenditures for labor.

County government was fairly primitive and one room and a few notebooks sufficed for its operation. The treasurer made his own arrangements for safekeeping of funds. The sheriff, clerk and school superintendent generally had farms of their own to care for and devoted only part of their time to public duties. When trials were held a room was needed and, if there was not one on a second floor over the auditor's office, then the ultimate demand was for a court house.

Usually purchase of a lot and erection of a frame building followed and the county got something resembling the Civic Garden Club building in LaConner. A plaque on it states that it was erected about 1875 for a grange hall, that it became the first federal court house north of Seattle, district court for Whatcom County was held there and it was the first court house for Skagit County.

Washington has 39 counties, five more than it had the year the state was organized. Missing from the list are four "lost" counties created inside the present boundaries in the early territorial period and five others which became parts of Idaho and Montana.

The true phantom counties were Quillehute and Ferguson, which existed one and two years respectively. Chehalis and Sawamish had somewhat longer careers.

At the founding of the state a law was written stipulating that no new county should be established which reduced the population of any existing county to less than 4,000 and no territory should be stricken from any county without a petition of the voters. This reversed early practices when a handful of men could promote a county of their own and fill its offices themselves.

Such was the vast county of Quillehute, extending nearly from Cape Flattery to the Queets River and inland approximately to the summit of the Olympic Range. In January, 1868 a little group succeeded in pushing through the Legislative Assembly an act creating the new county out of parts of Jefferson, Clallam and Chehalis. Every member of the group got an appointment out of the maneuver. Even then insufficient settlers were attracted to the wilds to complete the roster of county officers and the act was repealed the following January.

Sawamish County, named for an Indian tribe, lasted somewhat longer. Its total population five years

THE OLD court house in LaConner.

after organizing was 150. In 1864 the name was changed to Mason County and the size was whittled down.

Chehalis County, now mostly Grays Harbor County, extended to Bruceport, which was the county seat. Paradoxically all of the officers were residents of Pacific County. It was a matter of convenience for a few. Its first important business was to defeat a liquor law. Its court house was an unused blockhouse.

Ferguson County was east of the Cascades and was named for James Leo Ferguson, a controversial member of the House from Skamania County. Ferguson County existed on paper only; it never was organized and disappeared from the books two years later, in 1865. Its northern part was annexed to Stevens County and the southern part became Yakima County.

One other county, Skamania, nearly joined the list of phantoms when it was wiped from the records in 1858, four years after it was created. Like Quillehute, it did not have enough residents to fill the list of offices. The tale is told that William M. Wilson, auditor, lost all his records except those in the pocket of the coat he was wearing when he fled to the nearest blockhouse, hotly pursued by Indians one March day in 1856.

Several years passed before the county regained both its dignity and an influx of population sufficient to warrant its restoration to the roster.

Grays Harbor County Court House was erected in 1911. Its location in Montesano was successively in Chehalis and in Sawamish Counties. The building embellished with murals and an ornate clock tower, has been the scene of many dramatic trials, among them that of members of the I.W.W. accused of killing four veterans marching in a Centralia Armistice Day parade in 1919. Federal troops guarded the building during the trial.

Grays Harbor County's court house is undergoing extensively renovation, but the exterior appearance of the old building is being preserved. It will be retained for court-oriented functions while two new three-story buildings beside it will provide space for other county offices.

Quarrels over where a county seat should be located occurred repeatedly in Washington. Usually one town would resort to means of kidnapping the records from its rival. Dungeness and Port Angeles, Snohomish and Everett, Oysterville and South Bend, Sprague and Davenport all went through this ordeal.

South Bend captured the county seat in 1893 after a raid by boat on the older town across Willapa Bay. The records were in temporary quarters until Pacific County commissioners authorized the present court house, completed in 1910. It is one of the most beautiful in the state and is surrounded by attractive and well-kept grounds. Its interior is lighted by an art glass dome 29 feet in diameter over a

**GRAYS HARBOR County court house in Montesano.**

rotunda. The roof is of galvanized iron with copper cornices and ornaments.

Pacific is one of the three oldest counties in Washington and its excellent records, going back to when it was part of Oregon, are a joy to researchers.

Columbia County courthouse at Dayton is the state's oldest. The county dates from 1876, but the court house was not erected until 1886. It has Civil War cannons in front of it, a widow's walk on top and a sunrise decoration.

Old records make it a repository of history. Prior to erection of the building the county experienced a lynching and vigilante rule.

When Lincoln County was formed in 1883 an effort was made to call it Sprague County after its most important town.

There were three contenders for the county seat – Sprague, Davenport and Harrington. Temporarily the records were in Davenport.

At a general election next year it was charged that Sprague recruited railroad men from Ainsworth and Spokane Falls to vote in its favor. Names of persons buried in the cemetery were voted, also passengers passing through on trains. The number of ballots cast in the town exceeded its total population. As a result arrests were made but no convictions followed.

Davenport had been handicapped by lack of a railroad and the best its citizens could do was bring in extra voters on horseback.

Offices were arranged in Sprague and county records were ordered moved. But Davenport had no intention of giving them up and got out an injunction against its rival. A call for help was sent out and men came in from ranches, bringing six-shooters, Winchesters and muskets – any weapon they owned. Citizens of Davenport dug a trench, threw up a breastwork and posted guards night and day for three weeks.

After that the defenders tired, the injunction never came through and gradually the extra men went home from the fortified town. Thereupon Sprague sprung into action. A meeting was held and a body of determined men was organized, led by the sheriff-elect, a cousin of Buffalo Bill Cody. Riding horses and driving wagons for the purpose of moving the books, they descended on Davenport and captured the records before the farmers could gather to oppose them.

A court house was constructed in Sprague in 1886 at a cost of $10,000 and the county seat might have remained there had it not been that a disastrous fire almost wiped out the town in 1895. In the meantime Davenport had acquired a railroad and that November it was voted to move the county seat once more. Sprague's court house was sold at public auction and later became an academy.

The town of Asotin was incorporated in 1888 when it had about 200 inhabitants. The county had been formed in 1883, carved out of Garfield County, and the town of Asotin was named as its seat and was the chief beneficiary. The new commissioners met in a store building. Then followed a scramble to locate county offices. One man offered his store, rent free for one year, also fuel, light, tables, desks and safe. Another offered his dwelling, rent free for a year. Each of these men would accept an appointment as a county officer and turn his salary back. The two offers represented rivalry between the old town and the new. In 1886 and 1887 Asotin

City gave up and business houses moved to the new town of Asotin, which after that incorporated.

By 1899 population reached 500 and among the new buildings was the court house, costing $6,000.

In the summer of 1936 it was destroyed by fire and Clarkston made an effort to gain the county seat. This was defeated. In 1936 a three-story brick building on Asotin's main street was taken over and used for court house. The insurance money was spent remodeling it.

The county seat of Douglas County, organized in 1883, was first located six miles southeast of Waterville. It was in dry country and water had to be hauled in. When necessity of a change was discussed J.M. Snow brought a keg of water from Waterville and presented it as an argument at the commissioners' meeting.

The town, laid out in 1886, already had had two names. The post office was secured as Badger, for Badger Mountain, but the generally accepted name was Jumpers' Flats, until discovery of an unfailing water supply caused the settlement to be christened Waterville.

The county seat was moved there in 1887 and two years later A.T. Greene, one of the prosperous land owners, built and gave the county its court house.

Toward the end of the 1880's Port Townsend citizens believed they were sure to have a railroad within a short time. Plans for expansion of business were everywhere in evidence, therefore it was in keeping that public structures reflect the glow of confidence in the economic boom. Up went a new city hall, custom house and Jefferson County court house.

Until that time the county had occupied the Enoch Fowler Building, erected in 1874 for a retired sea captain and merchant. It is today the state's oldest two-story all-stone building and is occupied by Port Townsend's newspaper, The Leader. The material used in it consisted of blocks of sandstone quarried at Scow Bay, a few miles from town. When

PACIFIC COUNTY
Court House, South Bend.

**PORT TOWNSEND'S Leader Building was the old court house.**

the rock proved porous it was covered with cement in later years.

So much for the old building, which had been occupied very few years as a store before being acquired for the county seat. In 1889 construction began on the large brick and stone court house on the hill, designed by W. A. Ritchie, Seattle architect. Its style is Romanesque, its basic material 400,000 bricks shipped from St. Louis. Much carved stone was used in the trim, the friezes, arches and the clusters of columns beside the main entrance. The finishing touch, installed in 1892, was the four-faced clock in the tower. It was made to order by the E. Howard Watch and Clock Co. of Boston. Each dial is nine feet in diameter and the bell weighs 3,500 pounds. Formerly the weights and counterbalances were wound by hand; now an electric motor performs this service.

In a day of such ornate architecture it is an interesting observation that this building was not wired for electricity until 1912.

Pomeroy is the only incorporated city in Garfield County. When Joseph Pomeroy reached there in December, 1864 and bought homestead rights the place consisted of the Pataha stage station. Only two settlers had preceded him. At first Pomeroy worked for the Wells, Fargo & Co. stage line, but in 1877 he ambitiously platted the town and, with a partner, launched a flour mill.

Present Garfield County was scantily populated. At first it was in Walla Walla County, but in 1875 it was in the segment which broke off to found Columbia County. Citizens rebelled at having to travel to Dayton to transact legal business, so in 1881 they formed Garfield County, naming it for the president who had been assassinated that July.

Pataha City wanted the court house and it was 1884 before the matter was ironed out and Pomeroy was in undisputed possession.

An interesting feature of the building is the gilded figure of Justice surmounting the clock tower.

Everett's mission-style court house is dwarfed by the adjoining county office building.

The Snohomish county seat was in Snohomish from 1861 until 1897 and for some years the court house was a two-story brick and stone structure on the site now occupied by that town's high school.

The court house, newly erected after the move to Everett, burned in 1909 and the Spanish stucco building succeeded it.

Okanogan County also has a court house dating from the time when mission architecture was popular early in the present century.

The first seat of government was selected in 1886, the three commissioners of the newly-created county meeting at the Perkins ranch three miles west of Riverside. They held their session in the corral to accomodate the crowd that gathered. Some men sat on the top rails and others on their horses. A vote was taken and Ruby, then enjoying a mining boom, was selected for the county seat. It remained there only eleven months, then moved to Conconully, where it stayed until 1914. By then the population was shifting and the court house went to Okanogan.

The domed building in Pasco, dating from 1912, is not Franklin County's first court house. The

**TODAY'S JEFFERSON County Court House.**

93

LINCOLN County Court House, Davenport.

SNOHOMISH County Court House at Everett.

JUSTICE ATOP the Garfield County Court House at Pomeroy.

original county seat is not even a ghost town; it is Sacajawea State Park.

There, at the mouth of the Snake River, stood Ainsworth, a tiny settlement until in 1879 the Northern Pacific selected it as the place for beginning construction of its line from the Columbia River eastward. The community was named for J.C. Ainsworth, president of the Oregon Steam Navigation Co. and later a managing director of the

ASOTIN'S court house once was a business building.

COLUMBIA COUNTY Court House at Dayton, the state's oldest.

FRANKLIN COUNTY Court House, Pasco.

railroad. It was a rowdy construction town consisting of one street along the river, with many saloons.

Franklin County was created in 1883 out of part of Whitman County. After completion of the Snake River bridge the population gradually moved away, the railroad station was closed in 1885 and that year the county seat moved to Pasco, where crews

had gone to work on a bridge across the Columbia. The new community grew rapidly, but in 1904 Connell tried to get the court house away from it, contending the latter was a more central location. Pasco interests are said to have persuaded Mesa to enter the race, thus splitting the votes and saving the day.

DOUGLAS COUNTY Court House, Waterville.

ANOTHER MISSION STYLE court house. This is at Okanogan.

# City Halls

FOR some reason city halls in Washington seldom followed the pretentious lines of court houses. The town for many years was able to make do with modest quarters and today you can find them tucked away on the ground floor of almost any type of business structure.

Roy, however, has a city hall of considerable age which probably better reflects the early concept of the seat of town government. The old peaked roof has a false front. The fire bell was disguised in the tower and the fire department was formerly behind the big door. Now it is in a separate building.

Roy is a very old Pierce County community, as it was on the fringe of the Hudson's Bay Co. sheep pastures and was settled with the first influx of Americans seeking lands.

Modest seats of municipal government were not for the boom cities on the coast around 1890. Bellingham, in the flush of its railroad promotion, erected an imposing red brick, presently the home of the Whatcom Museum of History and Art.

At that time Bellingham consisted of four separate towns – Whatcom, New Whatcom, Sehome and Fairhaven. New Whatcom had great aspirations and in May, 1893 it completed a city hall large enough for a community many times its size. The first legislative act in the new building was passage of a city ordinance to restrict cows from walking on the streets between 7:30 p.m. and 6 a.m.

By 1904 the newly organized city of Bellingham took over the three-story red brick building and the other towns were absorbed into the municipality. The structure did duty until 1939 when the city offices moved into more modern quarters. With considerable effort on the part of citizens the museum was settled in the Victorian building and all was going well until a fire, caused by defective wiring, closed it in 1962. The conflagration destroyed the left front cupola and the center tower in which there had been a clock with four faces.

At first it looked as though that was the end of both the city hall and the museum, but citizens and the municipality conducted a long campaign to raise funds for restoration. When the building reopened to the public the clock tower was gone, but the missing front cupola was replaced.

A local art authority was once quoted as saying of Tacoma's City Hall, "It's supposed to be a copy of the Palazzo Vecchio in Florence. It's a very poor one."

It and the round tower of the Northern Pacific Building, just across Pacific Street, were the most striking objects on the Tacoma skyline for a long time, as they stood on an eminence overlooking the port.

The City Hall was completed in 1893 at a cost of $200,000. It is of light colored pressed brick with dentils and cornices in the Italian style and an elaborate arched and bracketed clock tower. The chimes which sounded the hours were donated by a loyal citizen.

This building is a monument to the period when Tacoma called itself "The City of Destiny." When the municipality moved in, the great depression of the '90s was at its peak and it would be a long time before any more spectacular building would be attempted.

**BELLINGHAM'S FORMER** city hall is a museum.

THE CITY HALL at Roy has
the remains of a bell tower.

TACOMA'S ITALIANATE city hall.

# Castles and Chateaux

**T**RULY beautiful are the turrets and towers of the Spokane County court house, erected in 1895 and designed by Willis A. Ritchie, who contributed much to glamorizing Washington's architecture of that period.

Called by one historian, the sleeping beauty's castle, it belongs less with court houses than with the Gothic public buildings copied after European chateaux and castles. Its inspiration was the sixteenth century chateau of Chambord in the Loire Valley, France.

The court house is of locally manufactured light colored pressed brick and tile. Few changes have been made since its construction. In 1920 the steps on the east side were taken out and the front door was placed on ground level. What had been the basement became the first floor. Other buildings have been added in the grounds to provide additional office room. The 200-foot high tower at one time had a clock, which later was removed as not contributing to the attractiveness of the structure. At night the tower is flooded with pink light.

Cost of the building and the adjacent jail was limited to $250,000. Ritchie submitted his plan in a competition and easily outstripped his competitors.

Willis A. Ritchie, born in Ohio, moved to Kansas as a young man. He journeyed to the Pacific Northwest in 1889, arriving in Seattle two weeks after the great fire.

At 16 he was apprenticed to a carpenter. He studied under an architect who was erecting government buildings and at 19 hung out his own shingle in Lima. His youth was held against him, but in spite of this, he became extremely active. He was living in Kansas when a depression hit and he moved west.

He remained in Seattle three years. As an unknown he put in a bid for the court house to be built on First Hill and won because it was the only fireproof plan submitted.

Other structures he designed were the Whatcom County Court House, Jefferson County Court House and those for Clark and Thurston Counties. He designed the original building for the Soldiers Home at Orting.

Ritchie went to Spokane in 1892 and the next year won the design for the Washington Building at the Chicago World Fair. Besides the Spokane court house, he designed the city hall as well as many large homes and buildings in Idaho.

The Review Building in Spokane, like most of the city's business structures, dates from after the fire of August 4, 1889, which swept 32 blocks in four hours.

On the day of the great conflagration the Spokane Falls Review was housed in what had been a Presbyterian church on the same corner where the present building stands. The church was far enough away from the flames so that it survived and publication went on interrupted.

The Review, founded in 1883, was by then owned by the publishers of The Portland Oregonian. They had plans for an impressive building, to cost $100,000. Before this was erected a rival morning paper, The Spokesman, appeared on the scene.

The new structure was opened with a great fanfare on October 24, 1891. There were speeches and on the next day a 24-page edition describing the building. Some 8,000 persons streamed through looking at it, riding the elevator and viewing the city from the windows of the tower. It was then the most conspicuous structure in the city, 165 feet high, with seven stories, plus a tower and peaked roof. The style was French Renaissance, worked out in red pressed brick and gray Montana granite. The interior finishes consisted of white Italian marble, yellow Siena and red Swanton marble, art glass, cherrywood, imported English tiles and bronze hardware. On the second to the fifth floors were 55 offices, to be rented. The newspaper occupied the rest of the structure.

Then came the depression of 1893, the Spokesman, for all its promising start, suspended publication and merged with the Review. However, the latter was having its troubles, the building had an $80,000 mortgage hanging over it, many of its offices were vacant and some of the tenants who were there stayed on without paying rent. The Review was losing so heavily its Portland owners decided to sell a controlling interest to William H. Cowles in 1894.

He had arrived in Spokane from the East the same month the Falls was dropped from the city's name. After Cowles took over the newspaper, it also underwent a name change and carried The Spokesman Review as its masthead.

Another French chateau-style edifice of the same year as the Spokane court house is Denny Hall on the University of Washington campus. It had a different architect, Charles W. Saunders.

It was first called Administration Hall and originally housed the departments of liberal arts, mines, chemistry, engineering, medicine and law. It had a library, book store and an auditorium seating 700. A description at that time told of three mahogany glassed-in wall cases along the east side of the main corridor, one given to the Badger Debating Society, the second to the Stevens Debating Club and the third to the Y.M.C.A.

The exterior of the lower floor was of sandstone quarried at Pittsburg, near Enumclaw. About the time the contract was let, the quarry went into the hands of a receiver and production was so delayed the contractors had to do the work themselves getting out the stone. (They had enough left over to build the small campus observatory.) Above the first story Denny Hall was faced with white buff pressed brick, with above it a heavy terra cotta molding. The roof was of slate with two turrets across the front and three promontories enclosing a group of arch-topped windows. Those at the

THE REVIEW BUILDING, Spokane, home of the Spokesman Review.

SPOKANE'S FAIRY CASTLE, the court house.

right and left bore the entwined letters "UW" and the center one was adorned with a scroll and star.

A cupola completed the building and in it was placed the 400-pound Denny bell, brought around Cape Horn in 1862 and used on the earlier university building to summon students to classes. It was old and rusty and from 1912 to 1919 it ceased to be heard. However, from 1919 on it has been rung for each Homecoming.

Arched windows surround most of Denny Hall's main floor and three arches give the main entrance dignity.

When it was announced the structure was to be built a contest was held to select the design and the winning architect received a $1,000 prize. Cost of the building was limited to $125,000.

After the Second World War Denny Hall was structurally sound but badly in need of repairs. The wooden frame was demolished and replaced with steel construction, reinforced concrete was poured for floors, walls and partitions and the roof was replaced. The new interior cost $850,000. The remodelled structure looks almost exactly as it had formerly, but the setting had greatly changed.

When Denny Hall was completed in 1895 it com-

DENNY HALL, University of Washington.

manded a view of Lakes Washington and Union and Union Bay. The regents then were talking of placing a boathouse in a wooded cove at the head of the bay so that the students would be close to rowing facilites. Today other buildings and tall trees hide the scenic outlook.

Tacoma in years past claimed to have the largest high school west of Chicago. Without doubt it must have been one of the most striking in the United States, for it looks like a great French Renaissance chateau. That was the plan, for it was never intended for a school, but a magnificent hostelry.

In the middle 1880's the large wooden Hotel Tacoma on the bluff overlooking the harbor was exceedingly well patronized and, with the coming of the transcontinental railroad there was an encouraging prospect of increased tourist business. Henry Villard, head of the railroad, suggested to Isaac W. Anderson, owner of the property, that the Tacoma Land Co., of which he was manager should erect an additional hotel. The first plan submitted was rejected, Villard declaring that Tacoma must have something better than the elegant Hotel Portland in the Oregon city of that name.

Villard placed the project in the hands of a Philadelphia architect and the seven-story structure resulted. The understanding was that the Northern Pacific would pay half the anticipated $750,000 cost.

When the railroad went into a financial collapse the burden of completing the hotel was thrown on the land company, which beginning in 1891 spent about $480,000 before pressure of hard times stopped the work. The roof was on the building, but the windows were boarded up and so it stood for several years. In 1898 a mysterious fire appeared to have been set by an arsonist. Quantities of shingles and other building materials stored inside burned briskly and within half an hour the whole interior was ablaze.

The ruins had stood about six years when a contract was let to tear down the structure. Some of the facing brick was removed to Missoula, Mont., to be used in a railroad station, and the company intended to employ more bricks for similar purposes elsewhere.

Tacomans were sorry to see the end of their dream and suggestions poured in as to possible uses for the building. It was brought out that the high school was crowded and couldn't the hotel property be turned to use for this purpose? Once the suggestion was made to the school board, the transaction was a speedy one. Building and grounds sold for $34,500. Then began a bitter controversy over putting the structure in order.

Men were set at work removing twisted steel and heaps of ashes and debris inside the great walls that were 3-1/2 feet thick at the bottom and 2 feet thick at the top. Frederick Heath, architect, drafted new plans and the building was completed in 1906 at a cost of $300,788.

An unusual feature is a front step cut from a granite boulder a glacier deposited on Fern Hill. The rock was dragged to the city by 26 horses.

At the west side below the school lay Old Woman's Gulch, which Heath studied for use as a playground. Its bottom was seven feet below sea level. Then came an offer from two men to construct a stadium in the hollow if they could hold a lease on it for ten years. Tacomans wanted the site retained for the public so subscription was proposed. Some fill was put in the hole, a large amount of earth was sluiced away and a concrete stadium seating 30,000 and covering four acres was the net result. It gave the school its name — Stadium High.

A souvenir of the railroad boom is the round tower building in Tacoma that was headquarters for the Northern Pacific and overlooked the railroad yards. It was new in 1889.

From this building to the passenger station Pacific Avenue was built up with "costly brick blocks from three to seven stories high." Tacoma went in for wide streets and gentle grades "so that a horse and buggy could go anywhere at a lively trot."

The tower, completed in the fall of 1888, was brick and iron on the exterior walls, had a basement, three floors and an attic. There were 53 office rooms and 19 fireproof vaults, one with every suite. It was heated by hot water. The cost was $125,000.

Among the offices it housed beside the railway was the Tacoma Land Co. It was one of the most striking architectural features of the city because of its commanding location. In later years it housed the city jail, health department and other municipal offices.

In 1893 the legislature appropriated money for a new capitol and the contract was given to a Spokane builder. He laid the foundation and then went broke after $85,000 had been spent.

The legislature upped the appropriation from $500,000 to $930,000 but there still was no capitol and the foundation remained an eyesore until 1910.

Finally in 1899 the legislature compromised and authorized purchase of the Thurston County Court House and its enlargement, appropriating $350,000 to be spent for the building and alterations. It added another wing at a cost of $475,000 and used the edifice for 20 years.

An early obstacle had been location of the capitol. At first Vancouver, Steilacoom, Port Townsend, Walla Walla and Seattle clamored for it. Then North Yakima and Ellensburg tried to get it. The last contender was Tacoma.

While debate about the capitol went on, Thurston County set out to build the handsomest court house in the state and to insure that it was fireproof. Joists were of steel, there was no wooden framing

**STADIUM HIGH SCHOOL, Tacoma.**

THE OLD CAPITOL Building, Olympia.

STONE FRIEZE at the entrance of the Old Capitol Building facing Stylvester Park.

below the roof and exterior construction was of sandstone. The architecture was Romanesque, with two turrets flanking the semi-circular main entrance on Washington Street. Sixteen broad steps led up to it. County offices were to have occupied the first floor, court rooms the second and the school superintendent and jury rooms, the third.

In the center of the building was a tower 150 feet high, with clocks on eight faces. Beneath them was an arched observation platform 76 feet above the ground.

This then was the imposing structure purchased by the state. Though it had been supposedly fireproof, it was hit by a spectacular blaze on September 8, 1928 and the octagonal tower was one of the casualties. The edifice was rehabilitated and used for state offices. It was again damaged by the earthquake of 1949, but still does duty.

The first session of the Legislature which met there was in 1905. It continued to occupy the building through the 1927 session, after which it moved into the present Capitol.

Victorians regarded buildings as symbols and endeavored to make them fitting for their uses. A bank would give an impression of stability; a public building was desired as an ornament to the community.

The castellated style was especially fitting for military buildings such as the one at Fort Worden, known as Alexander's Castle, erected in the period between 1886 and 1890. The Army used the tower for family quarters. An Episcopalian minister once lived there. It was also a tailor shop and an observation post.

Victorian prisons were made to look like

FORMER ADMINISTRATION BUILDING, State Penitentiary, Walla, Walla.

LORD HALLETT'S house at Medical Lake.

medieval fortresses and at a distance resembled baronial castles. It was thought they should impress the viewer and have solemnity. An example is the old Administration Building at the State Penitentiary in Walla Walla.

It was constructed in 1908 of bricks manufactured by inmates on the grounds. Today it contains a store for the prisoners, employes' snack bar, barber shop, offices, visiting room, mail room and storage space. At one time the third floor was used for housing single custodial officers who wished to live on the grounds.

The enclosed passageway leads to the new administration building. Some structures on the penitentiary grounds go back to 1886, 1888 and 1891.

Few persons built castles to live in, but there were rare exceptions where a family did not mind appearing to dwell in feudal style, such as the Hallett House at Medical Lake. Its owner was an English nobleman, Lord Stanley Hallett, who was the town's first mayor. Spelled out in the brick on one side are "Hallett" and the date 1900.

This house took three years to build. Its walls are from two to four feet thick. A ball room occupies the third floor. Rounded brick newel

ALEXANDER'S CASTLE, Fort Worden, Port Townsend.

103

Truly a castle in appearance is the stucco-coated apartment house at 207 Walnut Street in Ellensburg, which has the distinction of having been intended for a governor's mansion.

In the 1880's citizens of that town were convinced their community had a strong chance of becoming capital of Washington, which was soon to attain statehood. Britton Craig, owner of considerable property, and his brother Samuel, a master mason, thought to offer inducement by laying out a suitable area for government buildings and erecting a dwelling worthy of the governor.

The house they put up was three stories high, the lower two of masonry and the upper one tucked inside a mansard roof. A cupola topped the out-thrust section in which there was a spiral staircase. The top floor had a ball room.

In 1889 Olympia became the capital and the Craigs were left with a white elephant on their hands. A mortgage on the house was foreclosed, but the new owner let the dwelling stand idle and it fell into disrepair. It changed hands several more times, on each occasion for less consideration. Finally Ralph Wiseman acquired it, remodelled the place, gave it the castellated look and converted it into apartments.

BEFORE RENOVATING, this building in Ellensburg was intended for a governor's home. Its wooden architecture was transformed with stucco.

posts on the porch stairs must have been hand chipped.

Hallett was born in Surrey, England, attended school in London and when he was 21 left for the West Indies. He went to California in 1873 and to Washington in 1877, driving a light rig north. He homesteaded at Medical Lake on the present townsite, then went to England and married his childhood sweetheart. He got into politics in 1884 and was elected county commissioner. Later he was instrumental in building Eastern State Hospital.

Mrs. Hallett died in 1888 and a year later he married her sister. That is when he was chosen mayor and in 1900 he went to the state legislature as a senator. Then the house was built to his own design. He had a trap door to the roof where there was an observation platform. Here he'd shoot off fireworks on July 4.

Hallett died in 1926 at the age of 75. His widow remained in the house until the federal government leased it in 1943, when it was remodelled into apartments for war workers.

McKEIRNAN HALL, Fort Wright College, Spokane.

# Railroads

OWNS followed the lines of railroads, which brought population as well. Railroads were really trail blazers. As one writer has said, "Agriculture and transportation established towns where fur posts of earlier days failed."

Trains could pull more than could be packed by horse or hauled by wagons.

Railroad land grants were not frowned on in the old days because everyone wanted railways. Land had little or no value then and the presence of a railroad was what made private property worth something.

It was 1871 before the first rails of the Northern Pacific were laid in Washington Territory, 25 miles out of Portland toward Puget Sound. Again in 1879 grading roadbed from Ainsworth east began. The main line was completed in 1883. The rails from Kalama to Tacoma were finished in 1873 and Tacoma to Seattle service began in 1884.

Railroad depots of that era were places of glamor and excitement. The most important hours of the day were when the trains arrived.

An overhanging roof with large brackets was part of railroad style, sheltering passengers without pillars getting in the way of opening train doors.

The old Northern Pacific station in Snoqualmie fits this pattern and is one of the most interesting

architecturally. It dates from 1890, when excursion trips to Snoqualmie Falls were popular with Seattle residents.

Special trains to the falls were made up mostly of flat cars with no tops and only benches on the sides. Passengers brought picnic lunches. The trains usually were 15 cars long and there was a delay at Issaquah on the way up, while the coaches were divided in two lots and the engine made a second trip because of the steep grade.

A place to see old trains is still around Snoqualmie, near which, the Puget Sound Railroad Historical Association maintains 16 steam locomotives and 49 freight, passenger and special equipment cars. It is having to seek a new home for them and for its mile-long track, mecca of countless sightseers.

The telegrapher, in the Victorian station, invariably had a species of bay window from which he could look up and down the tracks. The red brick depot at Oakesdale, Whitman County is one of a series very much alike on what was the Great Northern line.

A busy person around a place like this was the station helper. One employee recalled, "Those were the days when the local freight had to be unloaded by hand, transferred to the warehouse and

**SNOQUALMIE STATION.**

**WAITING FOR** the Puget Sound Railroad Historical Society train. Here an old-time scene is repeated.

YAKIMA STATION.

VANCOUVER STATION, built in 1907.

then put out for the town deliveryman to take to the final destinations.

"The freight might include empty milk cans, chicken crates, groceries, farm implements, gasoline in 54-gallon drums, and barb wire."

There was no railroad in the Yakima country until 1885 and, when the line was built, the Northern Pacific could not secure enough land for sidetracks and other purposes, therefore it started North Yakima, which is the present city.

Meanwhile an older town had been platted in 1870 a few miles down river and the court house was there. Legal steps to compel the railroad to recognize it failed.

The first railroad station was a box car squarely in the middle of Yakima Avenue, surrounded by sagebrush. In the end the city got its depot, described as "magnificent" in the booster literature of the day.

Presence of water often was the deciding factor

in locating a new town on the railroad. For instance, a station was to have been put in several miles from Reardan, but the residents clubbed together and dug a deep well to get the town where they wanted it.

A water stop is what they called the town with a tank beside the tracks. Some were surprisingly small, such as the little fellow on the Spokane, Portland and Seattle line at Plymouth, Benton County. The railroad has been re-located to a higher elevation on account of Columbia River dams.

An offer was made to move all the merchants from Yakima City to the new site and give them business locations of equal value. In the end almost everyone took advantage of this proposition and that spring the town took to wheels. Some buildings were placed on wagons of the type used by loggers. Others were pulled along on rollers. Some smaller structures were moved on railroad

CLOSED NOW is this Milwaukee Road station at Tekoa.

THE TELEGRAPHER sat inside this window at Oakesdale, Whitman County.

cars. The First National Bank had its brick vault trundling along for three days and did business all the time. Goods were sold in stores, boarders ate meals and church services were held while the buildings were on the move, some for nearly a month.

At Roy the old railroad water tank is kept in repair today by the town's fire department. The tank is of wood construction and is among the many interesting souvenirs of early times which abound in the community.

**BUT FOR THE FIRE DE- PARTMENT at Roy acquiring this railroad water tank, it would have disappeared like most of its contemporaries.**

**WATER TOWER at Plymouth on the former line of the Portland, Spokane and Seattle Railroad, which has been relocated to a higher elevation.**

**MODERN GRAIN STORAGE tanks of the elevator at Prescott overshadow the Union Pacific station.**

# Water Towers and Windmills

WHEREVER the tower remains of an old water exist in Western Washington one can be almost positive there once was a windmill. The wind furnished the oldest means of pumping.

Windmills were first heard of in the seventh century in Persia. They were used to pump water to irrigate gardens and for power to grind grain. Nothing better had been invented for country dwellers when immigrants were moving into the western United States so they copied the source of power which they had always known.

Steam engines and petroleum-fueled motors were for the cities; the wind was a cheaper helper. Settlers in the new country could not afford expensive towers, such as the mills with great sweeps which are still to be seen preserved on Long Island, N.Y.

Daniel Halladay was the originator of the small round fan made of tiny wooden slats, with a tail to set it going in the breeze. This was the kind of windmill that first reached Washington. It usually perched atop the clapboard water towers now mouldering among old farm buildings. For some reason the owners liked them painted red.

In 1883 Thomas O. Perry designed more durable sails made of steel and set them on top of metal towers. A furl wire at the base of the tower permitted the sails to be set in the wind and was the only control needed.

East of the Cascades on the huge old ranches are the remains of numerous windmills of this type, gaunt and battered relics of the days when no power lines crossed the country and a farmer's

**THIS WATER TOWER seems to have a close affinity to horses, in fact it looks as though blacksmithing had been done there. It is at Coulee City.**

**REMAINS OF a windmill north of LaConner.**

108

A WINDMILL and water tower at Edgewood, Pierce County. Both are out of action but continue to serve as reminders of a picturesque past.

water troughs for stock had to be kept filled from the deep wells. There were then no gasoline pumps or electric switches to carry on the work.

In some distant parts of the world the spinning silver fans still are used, but in Washington, where there is no lack of power, the picturesque windmill is a thing of the past.

Relegated to the past like windmills were the pumps that formerly provided water for kitchen and livestock, and too often imparted a taste of iron to the precious fluid.

There is another kind of water tower, that for supplying cities. Rarely do these rate attention, but Seattle has one in Volunteer Park that is really good to look at because of its classical lines. It was completed in 1908 and serves a double purpose, having stairs and an observation platform on top.

The site of Volunteer Park was once held by the Washelli Cemetery Co. It was obtained by the city in 1887 through a court order, condemning a 40-acre tract. This was Lakeview Park until the present name was suggested in remembrance of the First Washington Volunteers, who served in the Spanish American War.

L.B. Youngs was supervisor of Seattle's water from 1895 to 1923 and six years earlier he had directed construction of the nearby reservoir. The new brick tower was supposed to honor him. It is 60 feet above the hill top and its observation platform is 510 feet above sea level. The tank inside holds 883,000 gallons of water, as compared with the reservoir's capacity of almost 20,000,000 gallons.

PUMP NEAR the county road between Colfax and Manning.

AN ABANDONED WATER TOWER at N. E. 135th Street and 39th Avenue N. E., Seattle certainly was not handed down from early days, but it nevertheless has the look of antiquity.

A LINCOLN COUNTY homestead, the house abandoned but its windmill still standing.

110

PUMP AND HORSE TROUGH in the historical park at Cashmere.

THE WATER TOWER in Volunteer Park, Seattle.

AN OLD PUMP supports a mailbox near Conconully.

THIS LEWIS COUNTY windmill is idle and the fence is moss grown.

# Water Wheels

OLDER than wind power was the water wheel. The first ones ever made stood upright in a stream like a turnstile, with grinding stones over them. Later cogged wheels were invented, permitting the paddles to turn horizontally in the stream.

Water wheels powered the first grist mills in Washington in Hudson's Bay Co. days and they drove the first sawmills. No miller or sawyer in the territory's initial years chose a location away from a rushing stream. A small dam and a flume were all that he needed for his wheel.

Washington was dotted with these quaint little mills for a quarter of a century or more, then with the improvement of transportation and the spreading use of electricity the water wheels fell into disuse. Flour milling and sawmilling expanded on a big scale and the tiny establishments on country streams no longer had markets for their products.

One still can find very old houses of boards sawed by a water-powered ''muley,'' an upright saw like that installed by Michael Simmons and fellow workers in the initial sawmill on Puget Sound. At first there were so few mills of this type the boards were floated long distances on the water and hauled through forests to construct the frame dwellings much desired by families from the East. Cedarville on the Chehalis River had such a sawmill, the only one on the entire length of the stream.

To find the remnants of a water-driven sawmill today would be almost impossible. There was one started on Blakely Island in the San Juans as late as 1910, but, if it had a wheel, the traces are no longer there, only ruins of the mill itself.

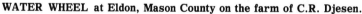

**WATER WHEEL at Eldon, Mason County on the farm of C.R. Djesen.**

THIS WHEEL WAS brought to Federal Way with other pioneer structures featured in the shopping center.

AT UNION, MASON COUNTY is a wheel built in 1900, which generated the first electric power on Hood Canal. Actually it is not the original, which was ruined in 1924 during a silver thaw. William D. Dalby and his son, Ed, replaced it with a wheel made from an old Yesler Way cable-car counterbalance pulley from Seattle.

AT DIABLO is the Davis ranch power house, erected in 1908. The Davis family pioneered on the Upper Skagit River.

REMAINS OF a water wheel at Lakewood, Pierce County.

# Barns

THERE used to be a barn near the Skagit River a mile and a half north of Mount Vernon that stood almost a century and was torn down only because the city limits spread out, took it in and created a high tax situation.

All the lumber that went into this great structure was brought down the river on boats and hauled to the hill site by ox teams. The owner, a minister, was raising hops and wanted to store them there, but when he discovered that his product went into beer and not for medicinal purposes, as he had been led to believe, he ripped out the vines. He went broke as a result.

The huge roof was upheld by a forest of upright timbers and crossbraces put together with wooden pegs, 42 timbers across the center and 32 other uprights. The dimensions of the barn were 125 feet by 85 feet. A cupola ventilator surmounted the central part of the structure. It flared out in all directions.

After the owner quit making money from hops he turned to Holstein cattle and horses, but was not so successful.

This man was ahead of his time with the Holsteins, the first in Skagit County. It was hard to sell milk; he delivered it in 30 gallon cans and measured it from his spring wagon.

In those days farmers didn't use stanchions. They had stalls for horses and sometimes for cows. Sometimes owners put storage space underneath a barn like that for vegetables.

Building a large barn was an important rural event, for such a structure usually was more imposing than the owner's home.

An 1877 issue of the Snohomish newspaper describes the enterprise of an early dairyman and observes that ''It is with pleasure we chronicle any efforts made in this direction.'' Then it goes on to tell how a certain Mr. Oliver provided suitable accomodations for his cows:

''This fall he has constructed a cow shed where he has now 16 dairy cows sheltered. The floor is so arranged that where the cows are placed in the stanchions they are always kept dry, all the wet draining from them. About half way between his barn and house he has erected a milk house some 13 feet square, with what carpenters call a hip roof, or a roof that slants downward on each of its four sides. This roof projects on each side some four feet beyond the walls of the building so that the sun can never strike the wall of the building. It is two feet from the ground. The room will be ventilated from under the floor, as well as by the ventilation established between the side walls and roof. Inside the building is to be lathed and plastered, the space between filled with sawdust, thereby securing coolness with cleanliness and perfect ventilation. With such arrangements it will always be easy to make a first-class article of butter.''

Dairying has gone through changes since those days. Delivery in milk cans was replaced by bottling, which had to be done close to the source of supply, otherwise the milk soured. It used to be picked up every day, but this is no longer the case.

High - temperature short - time pasteurization gives it greater keeping quality, so it does not have to be picked up so frequently. With refrigerated farm tanks, the milk is cooled and can be hauled long distances, yet less of it sours than in the past.

Now the stanchions for milking in the barns have disappeared, and very few large herds are kept in them. Instead the cows are in a loafing shed and feed is brought to them. Modern farms have milk parlors where eight cows can be milked at a time. An electronic feeder works while the milk is flowing.

The pioneer in Snohomish County with his 16 head of dairy stock could not make a living today. A man with less than 100 head had better get out of the business. If he has inherited one of the great barns on his farm, he generally uses it for hay storage or converts it into a loafing shed. No longer do we see dairy cows grazing in the field unless they are out there to freshen.

A manufacturing aspect of dairying also has changed. There used to be ten or more condensaries west of the Cascades and considerable of this product was shipped for export. Of these condensaries only two remain and export milk is going

THE SPRAWLING BARN of a farm near Lake Roosevelt.

out in the form of solids, which are reconstituted into milk with the addition of cocoanut oil.

So the barns are monuments to a time long past. Architecturally they were interesting, especially as to cupolas, which were really roof ventilators. Each farmer seemed to have chosen to express his special taste in them.

Completion of a big barn often was signaled with a country dance.

Rarely there have been round barns. Such structures may have had a religious origin. There was a saying that a round barn would keep the devil from hiding in the corners.

Silos as a general rule were added in the 1900s. There were none anywhere before 1873. Earlier storage was in holes in the ground, copying the Indian corn cellar.

The oldest silos were a skin of light boards held together with wires and hoops. Many leaned in the direction the last storm had blown.

In the grain country, before the coming of harvest machinery, wheat was pounded on the barn floors with flails, a noisy occupation.

Building a barn was among the first considerations of the pioneer, for his farm animals needed shelter. A cow was soon acquired, if not already owned, to provide milk and butter. Washington's dairy industry had small beginnings and not a few bovines went to their new wilderness homes, ferried up a coastal river by Indian canoe.

There was another kind of barn, the stables one found in towns served by stage and mail lines. The barns were a prosperous business, serving as the terminus of a freight or mail run. The driver would rest for the night, feed his horses and return next day. Traveling salesmen, "drummers" in the parlance of that era, used to rent rigs for as much as three weeks at a time and travel over the country.

In 1887, the year of the big snow in Eastern Washington, four feet fell at Goldendale and on the last night of the storm the rafters of the town's big barn creaked and moaned and the roof showed a visible sag. It sheltered 100 head of livestock and 25 or 30 men were sleeping in the hay mow under the roof. It was imperative that the building be saved from collapse, so the owner organized a crew to shinny up and shovel off the snow, a cold and miserable job, but it accomplished its purpose.

COACH BARN near Tukwila.

SILVANA DAIRY BARN with ornate cupola.

THE GREAT ROUND BARN on the Richard Hall ranch, one mile west of Steptoe, Whitman County, is 68 years old.  The dark cone in the background is Steptoe Butte.

BARN AT A stage-coach meal stop at Bodie in Okanogan County.

DAIRY BARN on Marble ranch at Grandview, Yakima County.

BARN AT Edison.

HERE'S THE KIND OF stable formerly in towns where for-hire rigs could be obtained. This one at Twisp later became a garage.

THIS PUGET ISLAND feeding shed is combined with a silo.

HORSE BARN at Reardan, Lincoln County, built at the turn of the century.

ANOTHER STYLE OF cupolas on this barn north of Carnation.

HERE'S A RESTORATION of the Fort Spokane horse barn, built for the quartermaster in 1884.

# Signs

BROAD expanses of walls on the old barns were an invitation to the painting of signs on them.

Business firms called them outdoor advertising, as the billboard people do today. Painters usually traveled around the Pacific Northwest putting on one sign only to a contract. Some were 80 feet long and 40 feet high and took the entire sides of buildings. They were paid for by the square foot — the bigger the sign, the more the itinerant painters received.

At stores usually its name was painted for the privilege of adding the larger lettering about the article advertised.

In the country often no money exchanged hands, but a box of products was given for payment.

Painting on the sides of Eastern Washington grain elevators in summer was a hot and trying job.

Roads were bad, there were many miles between the places where the men painted, so they carried a little fly tent, a ladder and a box of groceries in their car along with a trunk full of paints and brushes. Some days they painted several signs, then none for several days. The company that hired them usually wanted a sign in every town — the bigger the town, the more signs.

The funniest sign a painter said he ever did was "Ha, ha, ha, it didn't hurt a bit," for a dentist who wanted eight of them around Bellingham. Another on a drug store read, "It's a pleasure to die after taking our medicine."

That was a seasonal job — you took to the road every spring. It's different now with unions, licenses and no available buildings. There was adventure to it. Sometimes a tenant agreed to a sign and an owner objected and it had to be painted out to avoid a lawsuit.

**PATENT MEDICINE sign near Waterville.**

**A BACON ADVERTISEMENT** at Tukwila on a barn so old it was put together with wooden pegs.

A BIG EXPANSE to cover on this barn near Waterville.

AT EDISON this barn has signs on both ends.

THESE TWO are in art glass in the Mutual Life Building on Seattle's Pioneer Place.

# Brick Construction

BRICKS have been known since ancient times and, because of the European influence, appeared early in colonial America. They were employed more generally in the East; pioneers used them little except in the Southwest where the country was barren of timber. Even there Spanish occupation influenced the introduction of adobe construction.

In Hudson's Bay Co. times bricks for chimneys were brought to Washington, for it was not believed that good clay for making them existed here. Company ships delivered those that were needed and, when more population arrived, American vessels brought bricks from the East Coast.

Eventually some bricks were made at Fort Vancouver and on Puget Sound the first ones were manufactured at Steilacoom in 1858 by M. F. Guess. He ran one kiln of 50,000 and then abandoned it. The next bricks in the town were made by Peter Judson, but after a season of no profit he retired.

Brickmakers here had expenses far too heavy for them to compete with the East Coast. Methods of preparing the clay and molding it were slow and costly.

The oldest brick building in Washington is at Bellingham. It was erected in 1858 of brick manufactured in Philadelphia and brought around Cape Horn in a sailing vessel. It served during the Fraser River gold rush as a combination store, bank and commission house. Whatcom County acquired the building for a court house in 1863 and it fulfilled this purpose until 1891. It was also for a time the jail for Whatcom, Skagit, San Juan and Island Counties.

After that the building housed a newspaper and it has been converted to many other uses, last of which was a taxidermy shop.

Bellingham Bay had other brick structures in early years. The first brick house in the territory was at Whatcom, built of bricks brought from San Francisco. Another house in the town was made of Japanese bricks.

A book published about Seattle in 1889, before the fire, said that during the preceding two years great progress had been made in construction of brick business blocks. In most instances the ground floor was for stores and the upper floors for offices.

After the fire bricks were more than ever in demand and by 1901 nine large companies were making them on the outskirts of Seattle. Thirteen brick plants opened on Vashon Island and barges were employed to bring in their product, also that of brickyards on West Waterway.

Bricks are heavy and it was slow work delivering them with four-horse teams. The difficulties in hauling were one of the reasons for scattered brick yards in various neighborhoods where clay was found — anything to get the bricks closer to the jobs.

In Spokane is an old building that must have been among the first to go up after the city's big fire. It is the Mark Soss Block, dated 1889, but not completed for another year or so. It was first called the Bodie Block. Soss added his name to the structure a good many years later, as he did not acquire the property until 1920 or move his second-hand jewelry, clothing business and loan office into it until 1933.

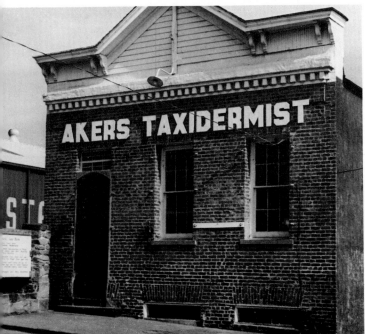

**THE OLDEST BRICK BUILDING** in the state, at Bellingham.

HERE IS 1890 architecture along the main business street of Dayton. One has to look up to discover it above the modernized store fronts.

THE MARK SOSS BLOCK in Spokane.

A REAL OLD-TIMER in Sprague with window trims and border of artistic cast iron.

THIS TAVERN AT East Heron and South G Streets, Aberdeen looks ornate enough to have once been a bank. Note the arched pattern in the bricks on the second floor.

123

# Windows and Cornices

IN the Victorian age many building tops were in Gothic designs or patterned after Italian palazzos. Many hundreds of commercial buildings with arched windows and strong moldings and cornices still stand. This was a style which began in the 1830s and was still popular at the turn of the century.

Bricks were employed to obtain all sorts of unusual borders. Sometimes the building was brick and the window casings were of stone. Arched windows were very common.

The peak time of the ornate structures seems to have been around 1889, just as the railroad boom period got under way.

An interesting building in Seattle was named for Austin A. Bell, only son of William N. Bell, a member of the city's founding party who landed at Alki on November 13, 1851 from the schooner **Exact.** Bell's land claim, adjacent to those of the Dennys and Borens, became the separate community of Belltown, later annexed by the city. Austin, the second male white child born in Seattle, started his life in a log cabin about opposite the site of the present four-story brick.

The cabin was burned in 1856 during an Indian attack. The father moved to California, returning in 1870 after his wife's death. In the meantime the property had become valuable and he erected several buildings on parts of it.

William Bell died in 1887, leaving a $400,000 estate. Austin, who inherited a quarter interest, was regarded as one of the wealthy citizens. He had been married six years, had an attractive home, good business, social and family connections and should have been a happy man, had he not been haunted by ill health. He sold out his business interests except for a real-estate office and made preparations to erect a new brick building.

On the morning of April 24, 1889 he went to his office not feeling well. He locked the doors, wrote a letter to his wife, drew out a revolver and shot himself in the temple. The note indicated he did not consider life with poor health worth living and expressed sorrow that he must take this way out.

Mrs. Eva Bell completed his planned building at a cost of $50,000 and placed her husband's name on it. The architect was Elmer H. Fisher. The structure, of pressed brick, dressed stone and terra cotta, was then one of the showiest in the city.

**PIONEER BLOCK, Colfax.**

**AUSTIN A. BELL BUILDING, Seattle.**

It contained 63 apartments, much plate glass, two store spaces on the ground floor and an elevator, then something of a novelty.

Rising higher than the buildings around it, the structure still stands as a memorial to the dour, unhappy man who planned it.

Pioneer Hall, at Madison Park in Seattle, has been designated a National Historic Site. It features late Victorian brick masonry and pressed metal ceilings. The walls inside are covered with pictures of Washington's early residents.

Beginning with statehood, the Pioneer Association wanted a suitable hall for its meetings and in 1902 a partial solution was reached when Mr. and Mrs. John J. McGilvra donated a lot on Lake Washington for the purpose. The property had a wooden building in which members gathered for dinners in relays, the oldest having priority for the first sitting. By 1904 it took several sittings to feed the growing crowd of pioneer lineal descendants. As diners finished they adjourned to Madison Park for a program in the band pavilion.

About 1908 Miss Sarah Loretta Denny left a bequest to construct a building for the association. The contract was let in 1910. Women on the advisory committee for the builders were responsible for the cobblestone fireplace in the main meeting hall and its sandstone mantel inscribed "Auld Lang Syne." The rooms were furnished largely with gifts of relics and household equipment of pioneer families.

A real landmark is Seattle's German Club at 613 9th Ave. Between 1898 and 1932 it was the United States Assay Office.

The first owner of the structure was Thomas Prosch, who had it erected in 1886 as an office building and entertainment hall. It was then next door to his home. Prosch was at the time sole owner of The Post Intelligencer, which he shortly afterward sold.

The club building has a classic columned entrance. Originally planter boxes adorned the upstairs windows and a gas light hung from a wrought metal bracket to illuminate the doorway.

**A LONG FACADE on Walla Walla's old Main Street.**

**PIONEER HALL, Seattle.**

Bay windows were of endless varieties on the older buildings. They hark back to when the comings and goings on the streets were of prime interest to the occupants of upper-story flats. Bays were also regarded as a means of securing maximum sunlight.

Port Townsend's Victorian architecture is noted statewide because so little of it has changed. Gradually some gaps have occurred in the rows of buildings because they were too expensive to maintain in safe condition. Most had been empty too long.

The Hastings Building, erected by Loren D. Hastings, was adorned with cornices, friezes and bay windows. Formerly the tower and roof were topped with ornamental iron. It was the town's most costly business building.

The tower had a pointed turret, but its roof became leaky.

Native stone was used in the structure and some local brick. Doors and sills were of native cedar. Heavy joists on the upper floors, 4 by 12 inches and 70 feel long, have been admired by carpenters who never see such timbers now.

An 1891 fire map lists the occupants as a grocery, gent's furnishings and on the Taylor street side near the back a cigar and confectionery store. Offices were above.

Originally it was planned to have a bank occupy the ground floor corner and for a time this was the case, with William Saunders' private bank there.

The Mint saloon was in the basement, part of which on the Taylor Street side is shut off to form a tunnel-like space. A few years ago it was advertised as a "shanghai tunnel," but the owner, a Hastings granddaughter, vigorously denied this and said it was used for stowing ship chandlery.

Whatever went on there, legend has it that in the 1920's a worker, called in to attend to heating problems in the building, discovered a man's body among the basement debris.

CUPOLA OVER a pharmacy in Ritzville.

ELLENSBURG'S ELTON HOTEL, built in 1889, has an attractive corner.

SEATTLE'S GERMAN CLUB, once an assay office.

THE HASTINGS BUILDING, Port Townsend.

# Pioneer Square

THERE would be no Pioneer Square in Seattle had it not been for the great fire of 1889. Prior to that the area was a hodgepodge of buildings fitted into the confused corner where the two city plats laid out by A. A. Denny and C. D. Boren and by Dr. David S. Maynard joined.

The wedge of land occupied by Pioneer Place never was on the first city maps. It was represented by a wide space in Front Street (First Avenue). Mill Street, or Yesler Way, was the dividing line between the two townsites. It had been Henry Yesler's skid road leading to his mill on the waterfront. The streets on the south side of Mill approached but did not quite meet those on the north side, creating a jog in each.

Yesler's mill stood on the west side of the present Mutual Life Building. He owned a narrow piece of land extending eastward and here his employes dumped wheelbarrow loads of sawdust until they had accumulated deeply. Within a few years a line of one-story wooden buildings occupied the Mutual Life corner, the signboards on their false fronts announcing dealers in stoves, drugs, bakery goods and meats.

Opposite the mill, across Yesler Way, where the Northern Hotel and Scandinavian-American Bank Building stood in recent years, was Yesler's famous cookhouse.

By the time of the fire the early structures had been replaced by office buildings. The first Occidental Hotel was gone and the new one stood in its place, on the triangular property that is now a parking lot. The open area in front of it, known then as Occidental Square, was illuminated with gas lamps on standards. Horse cars swung around the corner, drays rumbled up from the wharf and trains went by on a trestle where Alaskan Way now is.

After the fire little stood in this section other than crumbling brick walls of a few gutted structures, such as the hotel and the Yesler Building, where the Mutual Life now stands. South of the square almost everything had been wooden and was completely consumed.

The city fathers concluded that one of the difficulties in fighting the conflagration had been the narrow streets and bad jogs around which traffic was forced to swing. It was agreed in rebuilding to widen all streets from 66 feet to 84 feet, eliminate the worst corners, raise grades to higher levels and extend Commercial Street. This extension created Pioneer Place.

Most of the buildings around the triangle went up soon after the fire. Their style is American Romanesque, with the Pioneer and Mutual Life Buildings remaining as the two best examples. They are notable for rich facades and carved archways.

Because of the massive rebuilding immediately after the fire and partly because of the influence of one architect, Elmer H. Fisher, there is great homogeneity of style and construction. Fisher was

THE MUTUAL LIFE BUILDING, pergola and totem pole. This open space was once known as Occidental Square.

ENTRANCE TO the Pioneer Building as viewed from the arcade in the little plaza.

responsible for the design of 54 of the new buildings, many of them in the vicinity of the square.

All rebuilt structures were required to be of brick, stone and iron.

Pioneer Block was completed in 1890. It had been started by Henry Yesler on the site of his former home before the fire. The deep excavation was there when the conflagration broke out and many occupants of doomed buildings hired draymen to haul their valuables to the hole and dump them in it, covering them with tarpaulins as protection against cinders and burning fragments.

As soon as possible construction resumed. Yesler was ambitious to erect on the site of his early struggles a structure that would rival any business building in Washington. It has a frontage of 115 feet on First Avenue and 111 feet on James Street and is six stories high. Formerly it had a central tower 134 feet above the sidewalk, but this has been removed. Perhaps it was a casualty of the earthquakes which damaged some old buildings around Pioneer Place.

Bellingham sandstone was used for the first floor and pressed brick, trimmed with terra cotta and sandstone, for the upper stories. Two columns of rough-hewn sandstone ran up either side of the building front and flanked the former tower. Between the columns on three floors are bay windows and the corner has curved bays extending up four floors. The main entrance was floored with tile and there were carved balustrades on the staircase.

Elmer H. Fisher was, of course, the architect.

The first floor was occupied by the Puget Sound National Bank and three stores. Their interiors were finished in Spanish cedar. Altogether 185 offices were in the building.

The basement was scheduled to have a Turkish

ANOTHER VIEW of the Pioneer Building. This shows the sandstone columns flanking the central portion.

CEILING in the Blue Banjo Restaurant, Pioneer Building.

WROUGHT IRON in Mutual Life Building.

bath and a barber shop, also an electric light plant and pumps for the water supply and for running the hydraulic elevator.

Work had started on the Pioneer Block in January, 1889. The fire in June damaged what was under way and the action of the city in enlarging the square necessitated changes.

Total cost of the structure was more than $250,-000.

The Mutual Life Building was erected in 1897, with an addition completed in 1903. It has a lower floor of rough-cut stone, with a heavy central arch at the entrance. Wide groups of windows are under arches across the third floor.

The structure has a solidly paneled entrance and lobby, ornamental elevator shaft, marble staircase and tiled corridors. The frieze above its entrance has interesting faces. With its addition the Mutual Life became a solid block 80 by 100 feet and six stories high. It had its own lighting and heating plant in the rear. A bank occupied most of the first floor and Mutual Life most of the second floor. It was pronounced "fireproofed throughout not merely in name but in fact."

The Maynard Block was built in 1892 at the northwest corner of First Ave. S. and Washington. It was the home of Dexter Horton's bank. The cornice was gone in the 1950s and the building was mainly vacant. It has an ornate entrance flanked with double columns supporting an arch with three decorative brackets and above them a stone-railed balcony. The first and fourth floor windows are arched. Below the third and fourth floor windows and above the fourth floor are dentiled friezes. The building is of brick and the lower floor of cut stone. A pronounced dentiled border is along the top.

The Cascade Hotel was built in 1890 and long ago was called the Olympic. Basement passages reveal traces of sidewalk many feet below the present street level and these are a favorite goal of "underground" Seattle tours.

As the streets in this area were regraded a bulkhead was constructed at each curb and the space between was filled with earth brought down from the hills and with debris left by the fire. Existing sidewalks were bridged to protect them from street traffic and to keep carts from falling off. This sometimes left lower store fronts to be replaced

FACES ON Mutual Life Building frieze.

ORNAMENTAL STAIR RAILING in Mutual Life Building.

THE WROUGHT IRON pergola in Pioneer Square.

FACES CAN ALSO BE SEEN in the ornamentation of the Maynard Building.

at new upper-level street grades. For some reason the builders of the Cascade Hotel left such passages intact and one may descend to the basement and walk along what was once the old sidewalk.

The hotel building itself has the characteristic stone arched entrance of the period, flanked by triple columns and on the third and fourth floors are arched windows. The corner has a curved bay running up the entire height. A frieze is visible above the second story.

The hotel is on the south side of Yesler, facing Pioneer Place.

The pergola, or arcade, on Pioneer Square was erected in 1909 when the little plaza was the terminus for two cable car lines and a transfer point for other cars going north and south. That was the year when tourists thronged the city to attend the Alaska Yukon Pacific fair and it was felt that some provision should be made to shelter them from inclement weather while they waited for cars. An underground comfort station was also desirable, but not everyone agreed on this point and its erection and that of the canopy, which would serve as a roof to the

stairs leading to rooms below, was vigorously opposed by the press and some citizens. An injunction against its construction was threatened, but one park board executive pleaded to build first and, if the structure wasn't liked, he would have it torn down at his own expense.

However, when completed, it was held up as the finest facility of its kind in the United States.

The style of the loggia is Renaissance, with cast-iron columns and bent iron brackets, cornice and ridge line. The architecture is slightly hybrid because the pillars, each weighing a ton, are of Corinthian design. The canopy contained 65,000 pounds of iron work. Total cost of rest rooms and pergola was $25,505.

When built, the structure was in the business center of Seattle, but this gradually moved northward and the district was frequented by careless and uninhibited persons who abused and misused the comfort station until it became a public nuisance. It was locked and the stairs were sealed in 1958. Today the picturesque pergola, wearing the patina of age, shelters several benches.

THE ST. CHARLES HOTEL just off the square was built in 1889 and probably is the oldest existing hotel in Seattle.

THE CASCADE HOTEL, once called the Olympic, is featured on Seattle's underground tour.

# Pavements

WEST of the Cascades wet winter weather could reduce roads and streets to sloughs of mud. Towns very early planked their main thoroughfares.

As far back as 1894 King County, as an experiment, gave the Seattle Brick and Tile Co. permission to lay 50 feet of brick paving in South Seattle at its own expense. Nothing happened as a result and it was not until 1912 that the county contracted its first installation of this type on the West Valley Road between Kent and Auburn.

Meanwhile in the late 1890s Seattle laid brick pavement on First Avenue from Yesler Way to Pike Street. This was after a sample block had been put down by the Denny Brick Co. The undertaking was judged successful and more paving was laid on Second Avenue. Then the highway from Seattle to Everett and the one south to Tacoma were surfaced.

Clay of the type needed for paving bricks was found on the south bank of Cedar River east of Renton and a plant went in that became the largest of its type in the United States. By 1908 it was producing 250,000 paving bricks daily and employing 200 to 250 men. This became the Denny-Renton Clay & Coal Co. and in its heyday it operated six plants seven days a week around the clock. It supplied all of Seattle's paving brick, sewer pipe and bricks for buildings in numerous cities.

Bricks were not the only paving materials tried out. In 1904 Seattle and Tacoma were considering paving with sandstone blocks, to give horses a better foothold on the hills. The stones, called Belgian blocks, for having first arrived on the Coast in Belgian freighters, were shaped by hand with a hammer having a blade at one end. Most of those laid in the two cities were produced in the San Juan Islands.

Another type of paving tried out was cedar blocks in Everett's streets.

The automobile dealt a death blow to the above methods of surfacing streets. Concrete pavement, as compared to bricks and blocks when wet, proved less hazardous for cars. Later asphalt took the place of everything else.

Occasionally one can still see stretches of the old hand-laid bricks or blocks. Some are visible beside Seattle's Olympic Hotel at Seneca Street and Fourth Avenue.

Brick sidewalks at Fort George Wright College in Spokane date back to when the campus was part of a large military establishment.

In 1894 it was rumored that the government intended to construct a military post somewhere in the area. Spokane wanted it but had a difficult time meeting the requirements calling for 1,000 acres of land, water right and $40,000. The fire had cramped city finances, but the fund was eventually raised.

By 1899, 17 large red brick buildings had been constructed on the site west of the city and housing

**SEATTLE'S PAST shows through its pavements. The blacktop at Seneca Street and Fourth Avenue wore down to the bricks underneath.**

132

was provided for two companies of infantry. The sidewalks and the shade trees belong to that period.

In 1941 the post was transferred to the Air Force, but seven years later that department moved all its operations to Fairchild base and the fort remained merely quarters for officers' families. In 1957 the fort was declared surplus and other uses were sought for the property. It so happened that the College of the Holy Names, a Catholic women's school, was seeking more space for expansion and the sisters were among the applicants for the fort. They acquired a 75-acre tract in 1961 and now their campus consists of the red brick colonial-style buildings around a green expanse that was the old parade ground. Young women go to classes in the buildings, regarding which general order to troops was once issued:

"There will be no shooting of buffalo from second story windows of the barracks."

Today the grounds are as trim as they formerly were. But when the nuns took over their new campus all detachable fixtures had been carried away by vandals, porches sagged, plaster was falling from walls, broken windows were boarded up and weeds had overgrown the hand-laid brick sidewalks.

There was stone pavement in Seattle as soon as the feeling prevailed that plank streets were too difficult for drays pulling heavy loads up the hills.

Most of the stone was cut either on Sucia, Waldron or Stewart Island. The sandstone of these locales was of different grades of hardness and some was used in structures such as the old Public Safety Building.

**RED BRICK SIDEWALK in Chehalis.**

**A BRICK HIGHWAY shows up a block north of 175th Street and a block east of Aurora Avenue.**

**BRICKS SHOWING THROUGH at Pike Place north of Stewart Street in Seattle.**

THREE SIGNS LAID INTO Seattle pavements. The Hub mosaic now is in front of a parking lot at Pioneer Place. The Lippy Building has changed its name and its old occupants are gone. The Hotel Berkshire sign also is in front of a parking garage on Second Avenue.

FORT WRIGHT COLLEGE, once an army post near Spokane, has brick pavement worth talking about.

SMALL TOWNS had brick pavements too. This is Stanwood.

# Lamps

SEATTLE, W.T. It is a very picturesque place . . . The town is lighted by gas and has all the modern conveniences of cities of ten times its population.''

So wrote a correspondent of West Shore Magazine in 1875. Seattle was the first place in the state to have means of illumination other than whale oil lanterns, tallow candles and coal oil lamps.

When Governor Isaac I. Stevens reached Olympia in 1854 citizens celebrated by setting their crude lights in windows on the main street to lend their feeble glow to the welcome. Five years later Portland, Ore. got its first gas and by the early 1860's there were gas lamps on posts in the business section, though pedestrians still carried oil lanterns on most of the streets at night.

Innovations were slow to reach Seattle and it was 1873 before the city council granted Dexter Horton, A.A. Denny, John Collins and Charles Burroughs the right to erect a gas works and lay pipes for illuminating. The firm, known as the Seattle Gas Light Co., built a plant at 6th and Jackson close to where the railroad depot now is. This was then a tide flat. The source of gas was coal, the first storage holder was of wood and the mains were similar to the wooden log pipes then used for water.

On New Years Eve 1873 the gas was turned on for 42 private users and five street lamps. It cost the city $7 a month for each street lamp. In 1882 the council required all lamp posts to be metal. The extra expense was $12 a post.

Rates to private users of gas were much higher than now, costing $7 per 1,000 cubic feet.

Meanwhile Portland began to talk of electric arc lighting in the '70s and by the end of that decade Thomas Edison had announced invention of an incandescent lamp and had perfected a direct current dynamo and system of distribution. It was 1880 before anyone saw them on the West Coast.

About 1883 the new kind of illumination was discussed in Seattle and the gas company group obtained a franchise to produce it. The identity of the firm was changed three years later and it became the Seattle Gas Light and Electric Co. Its first electricity was generated from steam from Frank's Iron Works. This was said to have been the first electric system west of the Missouri. By 1889 Seattle's streets were lighted by electricity, both arc and incandescent.

The Seattle fire wiped out both gas and electric plants, but they rebuilt immediately. The company suffered financially and had to reorganize. By then it also was operating street cars.

Tacoma secured gas light early because better illumination than hand lanterns was needed for the hazardous climb from boats up to the town. The gas works were built in 1884. Tacoma got electricity in 1887.

Walla Walla's first street lights were installed in 1887. They were gas flares, lighted one at a time with a torch and snuffed out separately after dawn. The first electric street lights were put up a little over a year later. It was stipulated that they were not to operate weekends, only 27 days a month. The carbon arcs cost $13 apiece to operate each 27 days.

In 1911 Walla Walla installed tungsten and incandescent lights, three to a cluster.

A gas light installed in Pioneer Place in 1962 is like ones that once lighted it. The gas company found the lamp standard in Tacoma and built the head to specifications.

The open spot in the city earlier was called Occidental Square. It was illuminated at night with a few square lanterns on posts.

ARCADE PLAZA gas light on the rear of an old Spokane building.

LAMP STANDARD in front of museum, Fort Wright College, Spokane.

GAS LIGHT in Pioneer Place, Seattle.

LIGHT IN Woodland Park, Seattle.

AN OLD LAMP outside the Rainier Club, Seattle.

OLD LIGHTS transplanted to Volunteer Park, Seattle.

TRIPLE-HEADER GAS LIGHT Karcade Plaza Spokane.

# Covered Bridges

WHEN the horse and buggy were common, covered bridges were a familiar sight in the United States. Books have been written about them, but today they are rare.

Washington had its share of these coyly-termed "kissing bridges" and at one time there may have been 20 or more, mostly on railroads. Probably only nine remain today. A picture shows one on a road at Dungeness years ago. The only place where a car can drive through a covered bridge on a public thoroughfare today is at Grays River in Wahkiakum County. Another on the Manning-Colfax Road, formerly a railroad bridge, has been sold to a farmer, who uses it for access to his property.

Bridges were covered to protect wooden spans as much as possible from the weather. Ten years ago the Milwaukee Road had a dozen on its lines in Western Washington. The division engineer explained, "Covered bridges were constructed originally as a matter of economics. They were satisfactory structurally and cheaper to build than steel ones. Most went up in 1908 and a few years after that. In unroofed spans the trusses were boxed for the same reason as the completely covered ones and had the same general appearance."

Speaking of bridges in this state, people have forgotten the days when there were no bridges at all and stages or wagons plunged down banks and forded streams. Some of the first bridges in Washington were trees dropped over a creek and covered with small logs or planks.

Wahkiakum County's span has given the name of Covered-Bridge Road to an offshoot of State Highway 830 officially designated 12C.

The bridge was built in 1905 and before its completion a September flood threatened to carry it out. At first the 156-foot span was not covered, but because it is of wood, this protection was added. Later steel cables were placed under it, also a pier in the center for extra support.

Before the bridge was erected farmers had to ford the river with their livestock.

Both the town and the stream of Grays River were named for Captain Robert Gray, who discovered the Columbia and sailed up it as far as this tributary. In the pioneer period small steamboats went up Grays River thrice weekly, carrying mail and supplies.

METAL-COVERED wooden bridge southeast of Pe Ell spans the Chehalis River. It carries the town's water pipe. The road leads to a reservoir.

THE GRAYS RIVER BRIDGE is the only one on a public road.

ANOTHER VIEW of the Pe Ell bridge.

THE COLFAX – MANNING BRIDGE, owned by Mrs. Ruth E. Lowe, was bought from the Burlington Northern Railroad to give access to her farm. It is the only pony truss type bridge in the United States.

BRIDGE at North Bend.

OVER THE MIDDLE FORK of the Nooksack River at Welcome, Whatcom County.

THIS IS AGAIN the Colfax-Manning Bridge at the Palouse River. It was built in 1922 and covered in 1928.

THE BRIDGE AT DOTY, used by the Chehalis Western Railroad, is 59 years old.

# Barber Poles

WE now arrive at the lighter side of life, the whimsies, so to speak, that brightened the pioneer scene.

Take barber poles. They are a rare survival of the days of the craft guilds, when an emblem was important to indicate a man's occupation. The spiral stripe went back to fifteenth century England when barbers were minor medical men and were incorporated as "barber surgeons." They were entitled to bleed a man, the common remedy for many ailments at that time. The pole is said to stand for the stick grasped by the patient to encourage the flow during the blood letting. Of course, the red line suggested blood and the white spiral denoted bandages.

Barbers eventually were limited to their present trade, but they never changed the shop signs which showed them as surgeons.

Census rolls do not show barbers among the earliest comers in the West, but with the growth of towns some did arrive. They required little space for their kits, not much more than what was required by a farmer to keep shorn – a pair of his wife's scissors, a lather brush, cup and an old-style razor, honed on a leather strap.

Here is an especially intriguing announcement from a pioneer newspaper. The cut accompanying it showed a man in a tub, with a shower hitting him from above and another stream of water spouting from a pipe:

American Chop House

Water Street   Port Townsend

The subscriber having completed his arrangements for a first class Restaurant is now prepared to furnish meals of the very best description at all times of the day or night or to furnish regular board by the day or week. Attached to the house are a

Barber Shop
and
Baths!!!

Fitted up with the latest improvements and furnished with the soft pure water from Major van Bokkelen's celebrated well. The patronage of the public is respectfully solicited.

Wm. E. Bowen

**THIS POLE** is part of the collection surrounding a museum shop at Long Beach.

**THE LYONS BARBER SHOP,** 216 University Street, Seattle. Jack Lyons has been in this same location since the early 1920's.

SHOP AT OAKVILLE, Grays Harbor County.

POLE AT 1519 First Avenue, Seattle dates from turn of the century.

ONE HALF THE POLE is on either side of the utility post. This is at Stanwood, where you can still get a bath in a barber shop.

HERE is an exceptionally fine pole in Sprague.

THIS IS ON Main Street, Walla Walla.

ANOTHER TYPE of pole in Spokane.

POLE IN ADA'S BARBER SHOP, Pike Place Market, Seattle.

SIGN COLLECTION in barber shop at 1519 First Avenue, Seattle. The two poles at right are genuine relics.

# Cigar Store Indians

**T**HEN there were the cigar store Indians! The red man was seen much in American art and literature in the nineteenth century. The most widespread concept was the commercial image relating him to smoking, which is understandable since he was the first user of tobacco.

It is curious that at the time Indians were being ruthlessly killed off in the West the use of these carved wooden figures reached its peak. They are today a rarity, avidly sought by collectors. A good proportion of those remaining are in museums. Those still in private hands are kept for pure sentiment; they have a high value on the antique market.

When Lutcher's cigar store in Walla Walla went up for sale early in 1970 one of its assets was such an Indian, bought by Jacob Lutcher in San Francisco in 1881 when he opened his business. It had been shipped from New York around Cape Horn.

The Indian stood on the sidewalk in front of the store. He survived the fire of '87 and remained there until the city council passed an ordinance forbidding obstructions on sidewalks. He was then considered out of step with the times and was consigned to the basement for storage.

A few years ago a Lutcher son, who still operated the store founded by the family, realized he had something choice in hiding. He brought out Chief Smoke and placed him on a shelf, where he became a fixture of the store.

**IN THE SEATTLE** Museum of History and Industry is the replica of a Sioux chief carved in Montana approximately a century ago from a solid block of white pine.

**THIS INDIAN GUARDS** a combination motel and store at Lilliwaup, Mason County. Very few cigar store Indians remain. There is one in Seattle Center's Food Circus.

# Bandstands

BANDSTANDS, even empty ones, suggest Sunday afternoons in the days before television. Many a small town had its band and these generally assembled for a concert certain Sundays in summer. And if there was a large picnic in the park a band seemed to be a necessary adjunct.

Parks are emptier today than formerly, when they were family centers of recreation. If a park was near the water another way of listening to the concert was to take your girl friend by canoe and idle offshore while the musicians played.

Bandstands ranged from the plain utilitarian type to the gingerbread ones of privately developed parks or more affluent communities.

Having a bandstand did not necessarily indicate that the community had a band. The structure seemed essential if a park were to be used for community groups and large picnics. There had to be protection for speakers from the rain. There had to be a place above the crowd from which they could be heard and where the ''Star Spangled Banner'' could be sung to open ceremonies.

If the park was equipped with a locked storage room under the bandstand here a few folding chairs for speakers or musicians could be stored.

Some towns indeed did have bands, for before we had radio programs, music in the community was taken seriously. March strains were popular; particularly the compositions of John Philip Souza were brassily rendered early in the century.

City dwellers had nostalgic memories of the valiant little German bands of perhaps half a dozen members wandering the streets, tootling music that drew rapt children and housewives with their pennies.

One of the first known photographs taken in Oregon was made of a celebration when Congress had voted for admission of that state to the union in 1858 – a year before it was actually accomplished. The celebration was spontaneous. What is interesting is the row of musicians in the forefront – 12 or 13 of them. One had a large drum, two had French horns; there were some trumpets and fifes.

In Washington in 1870 we find a benefit ball was given for the Olympia brass band and the next year, a newspaper informs us, the musicians gave a performance ''from the water,'' presumably aboard a boat. Next we learn that the Olympia cornet band held a picnic and clam bake.

In that same decade Port Gamble, Seattle and Port Blakely organized cornet bands and Port Townsend got a brass band. By 1889 Kent had a band and Dayton had one of 27 pieces.

Musical news notes of the 1890s refer to Tumwater's brass band, Olympia's park band, which could have been its Capital brass band, the Harmony brass band, the reorganized marine band or the new Olympia Cornet Band. Olympia had all of these!

Ritzville, with its German population, had a brass band in 1900.

THIS STAND in Port Townsend was erected by the Women's Civic Club in 1905. The Whidbey Island ferry is in the distance.

CLARK PARK, Everett.

**THE CITY CENTER PARK** band stand in Centralia is close by the town's Carnegie Library.

**PIONEER PARK,** Walla Walla.

**FORGOTTEN AND FORLORN** at the end of a road west of Mabton, stands this split-level bandstand.

**ROCK MOSAICS** went into this bandstand in Causland Park, Anacortes. A lot of patience was expended on this one.

# Ice Cream Parlors

ETAL chairs and tables were invariably associated with ice cream parlors. Teen-agers took girl friends there after school sports events or programs. In cities it was accepted that following a matinee one went for a dish of ice cream or a soda. Thrifty children clutching a pair of nickels were known to ask for "one ice cream and spoons for two."

The ice cream parlor was a favorite retreat of the young. Romance thrived over sundaes. Ordering a banana split was a mark of opulence.

Seattle's first soda fountain was installed by William Meydenbauer in his bakery.

In the '90s and on into the present century ice cream was a home product, made in freezers turned by hand. Ice arrived by wagon and was tonged into the house to be stored in an ice box. Or in the country it was retrieved from an ice house, the crystalline blocks having been cut in winter from the top of a pond.

Arrival of the ice wagon was a time of treats for city children, who thronged around the delivery man, begging for a chip to suck.

To make ice cream in a home freezer the mix was placed in a heavy can surrounded by chipped ice sprinkled with coarse salt. A gadget at the top of the can braced it in the tub and supported a crank that turned the paddle inside the can.

Ice cream had to be eaten soon, no matter what its source, for there was no refrigeration. The creamery wagon that might deliver it carried ice and rock salt. The ice cream was packed in big five-gallon cans.

THE SWEET BEE ice cream parlor in Okanogan is equipped with a player piano.

# Hitching Posts and Rings

THE day of old Dobbin is gone, doomed to oblivion by the horseless carriage, and few reminders are left of his era. Usually these are in the form of cast-iron hitching posts saved by some fancier of horsey antiques.

Not every one could afford one of these jockey statues or made provision for a cement post with ring. Commoner was a simple iron ring set in the curbstone.

The average house had no such convenience and the usual expedient was for the horse-and-buggy visitor to tie the reins to a tree in the parking strip. Business and professional men depending upon buggy transportation carried with them a heavy iron disk to which a long strap was attached and this was dropped when the person reached his destination. Its weight effectively deterred the animal from straying.

Runaway teams were the terror of the streets before the advent of the automobile. The average horse, however, did not frighten easily. While his owner tarried the animal munched grass beside the curb or, if it were noontime, enjoyed oats from a bag slipped over its head. On hot summer days this same docile equine, pulling a grocer's delivery cart, might wear a peaked straw hat with holes for its ears to stick through.

Everything came to houses in horse-drawn vehicles – the fuel dealer's loads of coal or wood, the vacationers' trunks brought by the drayman, the butcher, the milkman, the baker, all had wagons and the physician had his smart rig for making house calls. And who would forget the vegetable man with his open wagon heaped with fresh produce and fruits? He appeared regularly a certain day each week. Cook or housewife – whoever did the family food buying – went out to the street to inspect his wares.

The row of rings shown in one of these pictures was located where it was customary for several teams at a time to wait, such as in front of the court house.

**PLAIN HITCHING POST** and mounting block on 14th Avenue E., Seattle. This shows the distance between the coach and the horse's head.

**ROW OF RINGS** in Chehalis. Modern parking meters now line the same street.

MOUNTING STONE in front of old Seattle mansion at East Valley Street and 14th Avenue E.

HITCHING RING embedded in a boulder at curb in Dayton.

A HORSE'S HEAD hitching post in Laurelhurst, Seattle.

JOCKEY HITCHING POSTS once were common. This is outside a Seattle antique shop.

# The Passing Scene

SO we come to the end of the road, to contemplate the things that are almost gone. Take Indian agencies, like the one at the bottom of this page, now occupied by offices of the Allied Tulalip Tribes.

At left is the base of a totem pole.

Then there were Carnegie libraries, mostly outgrown by the towns that have them. The one in Wenatchee has already served a long time as a museum.

Disappearing from the Central Washington scene is the hand-operated hay loader. For some reason, when viewed at a distance around Ellensburg they used to suggest old Hungarian well sweeps.

A loader still operates at Winthrop.

Not all of the ornate street clocks are relegated to the country as is the one on the Schafer estate in Grays Harbor County. It once stood at Fifth and Pine, Seattle.

There are still clocks in cities as big as Seattle and Spokane but they are very few in number. One in Anacortes has gaslight globes.

Then there are the things that were done with wrought iron. We have modern machine-made versions, but little of the kind of metalwork that came down from the gingerbread era.

Down to earth, one might say, was the iron boot scraper. The photographer found one at the Simpson Logging Co. office in Shelton. It's a reminder of the great gobs of mud loggers used to track in. Householders and businesses weren't above having such a scraper beside the front door.

Earthier still is the root cellar. The photographer went to the Okanogan highlands to find one east of Oroville. It outlived a farmhouse, long since gone.

Constantly today one is faced with the question - is this worth saving?

The answer lies with the individual.

While the state of Washington is relatively young, it has had precious landmarks that have been in the path of destruction. Often they were not so recognized until they were irretrievably lost.

In the several years while the pictures for this book were accumulating Victorian business blocks were demolished in Tacoma and Port Townsend, a graceful church was moved and deprived of its steeple on San Juan Island, and a covered bridge was torn down at Elbe.

There is a casual willingness in this country to destroy the old, and even the almost new. This tendency has deprived the nation of most of what was best in its nineteenth century architectural accomplishment. Perhaps our cities and our towns, one writer says, cannot afford a past except in the rarified context of museums, libraries and national monuments.

A few reminders are still around, not always noble architecturally or culturally, but nevertheless a picturesque part of our heritage.

The End

SCENE on Tulalip Indian Reservation.

CLOCK on Schafer estate.

HAY LOADER near Winthrop.

WENATCHEE'S former Carnegie Library.

BOOT SCRAPER, Shelton.

IRON FENCE, Port Townsend.                    INTRICATE IRONWORK, Black Diamond.

152

SASSAFRAS IS STILL LISTED on this striking signboard in the Pike Place Market, Seattle. The person who designed it was a bit weak on spelling.

ROOT CELLAR east of Oroville.

Sunday morning interlude, Skykomish.

Decorations
on building
in Prosser
(1903).

UNIQUE DOOR in the entrance to the Waitsburg City Hall.

**TOWER BUILDING erected in Tacoma in 1889 as offices for the Northern Pacific Railroad and later used as police headquarters.**

# Index